D0560310

HOW TO WIN AN ELECTION

HOW TO WIN

STEPHEN C. SHADEGG

AN ELECTION

The Art of Political Victory

TAPLINGER PUBLISHING CO., INC., *New York*

HOW TO WIN AN ELECTION

Copyright © 1964 by Stephen C. Shadegg

All rights reserved. No part of this
book may be reproduced in any form except in connection
with a review in a newspaper or magazine without
the permission in writing of the publisher,
Taplinger Publishing Co., Inc., 119 West 57th Street,
New York, New York 10019

Published simultaneously in the Dominion of Canada
by Burns & MacEachern, Ltd., Toronto

Published June 1964
Second Printing July 1964

Library of Congress Catalogue Card Number 64-20479

Manufactured in the United States of America

*To my children—Cynthia, Eugenia, David and John—
who in their years of childhood accepted without question
or criticism my weeks and months away from home, the
price they paid for my participation in managed elections.*

CONTENTS

ACKNOWLEDGMENTS

This book is the outgrowth of thirty years of experience as a participant in the battle for ballots. I am deeply indebted to many members of the United States Congress for the privilege of working on their campaigns and for the individual contributions they have made to my understanding of the mechanics of election presented in this book.

My gratitude goes to the Honorable Carl Hayden of Arizona; that entire class of 1960 Republican Senatorial candidates: the Honorable Gordon Allott of Colorado, the Honorable Clifford Case of New Jersey, the Honorable John Sherman Cooper of Kentucky, the Honorable Carl Curtis of Nebraska, the Honorable John Davis of North Dakota, the late Honorable Henry Dvorshak of Idaho, the Honorable Karl Mundt of South Dakota, the Honorable Leverett Saltonstall of Massachusetts, the late Honorable Andrew Schoeppel of Kansas, the Honorable Margaret Chase Smith of Maine, the late Honorable Keith Thomson of Wyoming, the Honorable John Tower of Texas; and, particularly, United States Senator Barry Goldwater of Arizona.

I must also acknowledge the gentleman who introduced me to politics, the late James Kirby, one-time candidate for the Democrat nomination for governor of Arizona; and to Sheriffs of Arizona's Maricopa County, Lon Jordon and Ernie Roach, now deceased, and Cal Boies. Many other along the path of this pilgrimage have helped to weigh and analyze the strategems outlined herein; particularly, Richard Herman of Omaha, Nebraska, and Richard Spelts of Grand Island, Nebraska; Bob McCaughey and Billy Morrison of South Dakota; Galen Broyles, Fletcher Swan and Jean Tool of Colorado; John Martin, Governor Robert E. Smylie, Jim Brown and John Corlett of Idaho; Russell Kirk of Michigan; Albert Fay and Tad Smith of Texas;

Chuck Colson of Massachusetts; Senator Thruston Morton of
Kentucky; John Wold and Hi Gernert of Wyoming; Sig Unander
and Wes Phillips of Oregon; and Robert Creighton, Frank
Riley, Orme Lewis, the late Clarence Buddington Kelland,
Jerry Poole and Alfred S. Hanson of Arizona.

I am deeply indebted to Oren Arnold of Phoenix, who urged
me to write this book based on my experience in political
campaigns, and to Mrs. Janice Maddern and Mrs. Herbert
Nelson, who did the real work typing the manuscript. Frank
Kelley, my friend and associate who edited the final copy,
brought great skill and tenderness to the task of sharpening the
words and phrases of How to Win An Election.

PREFACE

Following my service as a special consultant to the Republican Senatorial Campaign Committee in 1959 and 1960, I was elected State Chairman of the Republican Party in Arizona. In that post I was privileged to participate in the meetings of the Republican National Committee and in regional meetings where Republican Party politicians assembled.

There is literature available outlining requirements for effective precinct organization. Books have been written to assist the county and state chairmen in performing what to every beginner is a totally unfamiliar task. If there is in existence an authoritative book dealing with those strategems and techniques which lead to victory in the battle for ballots, I have never found it.

The necessity for this book became apparent when I spoke to the Western States Republican Conference in Sun Valley, Idaho, in the Fall of 1961. At that meeting there were gathered all the leaders of the Republican Party in the Western states. The techniques and viewpoints which I expressed were totally new, totally unfamiliar, to these men and women whose energies and abilities were committed to the task of winning elections.

Hopefully, the publication of this material will enable the serious student of politics to find a new perspective, to reach a better understanding of the problems and to be more effective in forming the political decisions that will shape the destiny of tomorrow's world.

HOW TO WIN AN ELECTION

1 | The People's Choice

The people of the United States of America will determine the shape of tomorrow's world. The sovereign voters of this Republic with their ballots control the most powerful military weapons ever developed, dictate the expenditures of more than a hundred billion dollars every year, decide the fate of nations and of people. The voters in America bear an awesome responsibility.

The man who is now President of the United States first won election to the U.S. Senate by a margin of 87 votes. The echoes of that political contest are still reverberating.

There is no prize for second place in a political contest. The margin of victory is not important. Once in office the successful candidate may move a little more boldly if he has enjoyed a tremendous plurality over his opponent. But whether the margin was 50 or 50 thousand the victor enjoys the power and perquisites.

Political campaigns which seem to absorb the attention and energy of the entire nation are soon forgotten. The loser fades into obscurity; the winner warms himself before the fire of public applause.

Nobody asks: how are elections won? because that stamp of

approval which goes with the majority opinion in a democracy smothers the question. What difference does it make how he won? He won, didn't he?

In the aftermath of almost any hotly contested political decision we hear the charge that votes were bought and sold. "Victory was the result of a political machine." A few examples can be produced to support these contentions of vote buying, but the truth is that candidates and campaigns are organized to spend money to influence the voter's ultimate decision. Every political victory is the result of organization and planning and unified effort. The objective of all political parties is to provide a powerful organization which on election day can give the party's candidate enough support to insure victory.

No one knows precisely how much money is spent each year on political activity. The present system of reporting is grossly inadequate. It is probably true that a minimum of $500 million is spent every four years on behalf of political candidates. Some observers put the figure as high as $1 billion.

A candidate for the U.S. House of Representatives, running in a rural district, might conduct an effective campaign on less than $50 thousand. But in the urban areas, and particularly in the big city districts, a race for Congress can cost as much as $300 thousand. And 435 members of the House must run for re-election every two years.

One-third of the U.S. Senate is elected every two years; senatorial contests are state-wide. They can cost as much as $2 million in California or New York. The minimum required to stage an aggressive campaign in a small state would be around $200 thousand.

Every four years we have a presidential campaign and each party, through its national committee, raises millions and spends millions.

The states must select fifty governors. In some states there is a gubernatorial race every two years, in others every four years. Add to these familiar political contests the races for attorney general and state legislatures, for various administrative commissions, and it soon becomes obvious that the $500 million figure is probably conservative.

Hundreds of thousands of individual Americans engage in political activity. 68,836,000 voted in the presidential election of 1960. The qualification for voting varies with the states. Out of an estimated adult population of 107 million people, 63.8% participated in the last national election.

After a national election, the commentators and the analysts engage in a great season of second-guessing. Many of their explanations are quite valid. The point is they are all made after the fact.

In football and baseball the coaches start with the recruits. They teach the fundamentals of the game until a shortstop, presented with a double play opportunity, moves almost entirely from reflex action. The quarterback with an option play knows precisely the choices open. The good quarterback makes the right choice.

In the field of politics there is no such opportunity. Candidates come in varying sizes and shapes. Some are well qualified. Some have almost no qualifications. Dunces and dullards have been elected to high public office. Some candidates move from victory to victory. Others are defeated their second time out.

The national political parties maintain offices in Washington, D.C. staffed with experts. The committees make studies and reports and offer what would be valuable assistance if the candidate knew how to apply the information supplied. Unfortunately, most of the candidates—particularly those without prior experience in the political field—don't have the slightest idea how to make use of the information supplied.

In the presidential years the national committee centers all of its attention on the party's presidential candidate. The man nominated by the party for the presidency has the deciding voice in the selection of the national chairman.

Long ago the members of Congress recognized the national committees as one-track-mind affairs and organized their own groups within the Congress to assist incumbent members seeking re-election. The Democrats and the Republicans both have senatorial campaign committees and in the House there are the congressional campaign committees.

These groups, organized to provide effective political assistance, are, so far as candidates for the House and the Senate go, far more helpful. But frequently there is a sad lack of coordination between the party's national committee, the party's senatorial committee, and the congressional committee.

The aspiration of representative self-government is to provide the people with leaders in political office who possess an uncommon competence. The theory behind popular election puts great confidence in the ultimate judgment of the electorate. There is an assumption that the majority opinion will elevate the nation's best to high office. Our political history seems to deny this assumption.

Politicians are fond of viewing a current election contest as being of supreme importance. In every election the future of life, liberty and property hangs in the balance. Political power in every public office has increased tremendously as we have delegated more and more authority to our elected officials. It is this very fact which makes each succeeding election increasingly important. As our involvement with the rest of the world increases, the political decision becomes increasingly critical.

The dearest persuasions of the past 6,000 years are being threatened. Our long-accepted Judeo-Christian concept of the nature of man has been effectively challenged by the doctrines of Marx and Engels. If democracy is to survive, if we are to march forward together into a better tomorrow, then we must soberly examine how political decisions are made, how elections are won.

What segment of the population makes the ultimate decision in any political contest?

Is the personality of the candidate or the political philosophy of the candidate the deciding factor?

Does the average voter know why he voted for the candidate of his choice?

Can public opinion be manipulated or controlled to produce a desired result in a political contest?

Does the average political candidate tell his constituents the truth?

What part do public opinion polls play in determining the outcome of elections?

In November, 1960, nine incumbent Republican U.S. Senators were re-elected. In Iowa, Jack Miller won a Senate seat on the Republican ticket; and in Wyoming Keith Thomson, a Republican, was the victor. In a number of these states the same voters who returned a Republican to the Senate chose John F. Kennedy over Richard Nixon for the Presidency.

This apparent inconsistency went unnoticed entirely or received only passing mention, the majority of attention being focused on the change in the national administration. Once the votes are counted very few people ever ask why this candidate was successful or why that one lost. Obvious anomalies, such as the election to the Senate of Leverett Saltonstall from Massachusetts—while Kennedy was winning the state by a tremendous margin—are dismissed under the general heading of "that's politics, I guess."

No two election contests are ever identical. No two candidates possess the same assets or the same liabilities. When a Republican candidate can sweep to victory in a precinct or a district where the majority of registered voters are Democrats, there is always a reason for the contradiction.

In our highly competitive world of commerce we have learned to view success objectively. We analyze the factors which mark the difference between success and failure. We

have learned that an aggressive sales effort frequently enables
an inferior product to dominate the market. We know that the
management of distribution and transportation will influence
the acceptance of one product over another. We know that in
some instances a company with lower gross sales will make
more net profit than the competitor who is outselling them.

In business the objective of all this effort on the part of
management is to make a profit. In all campaigns the objective
is to influence the voters to make a decision favorable to the
candidate.

The introduction of a new commercial product is usually
preceded by a very careful market analysis. The merchandiser
wants to aim at customers who have a need or a use for the
product, who are in an economic position to purchase the product. The approach is made through a proven medium capable of
reaching the consumers who are potential purchasers of the
particular product being offered.

In political campaigns such a practical approach is the exception, not the rule. Candidates and campaign managers—
much like Mr. Leacock's famous horseman—ride off in six
different directions all at once. Candidates waste hours of
valuable time expressing their favorite views on subjects which
have little interest to the potential customer—the voter.

There is a market for ideas and concepts just as there is a
market for girdles and mink coats. The campaigner who fails
to aim his remarks squarely at the major interest of his audience is engaging in non-productive exercise.

In politics the candidate is the product. He may be superior,
average or inferior. Voters are emotional as well as rational
creatures. They refuse to conform entirely to any set pattern or
to respond invariably to any particular formula. But, with few
exceptions, it can be said the body politic on any election day
is more influenced by the campaign than by the candidate.

To the uninitiated it might seem impossible to separate the
two. The citizen whose interest in politics is casual and passing

will declare that the candidate is the campaign, that what the candidate did and said is responsible for the voter's decision.

But what did the candidate say? Where did he say it? How was it said for him?

"I liked what the candidate said," says the voter.

Yes, of course you did. But why did he say it? When did he say it? How did it happen that you were listening?

"That fellow came to my town and I could tell he was interested in my problem," says the voter.

Yes, of course you could. But how did it happen that on that particular day the candidate managed to address himself to your problem and to speak in a language you could understand and accept?

"I didn't like what his opponent was saying about him, so I voted for the guy," says the voter.

Of course you didn't like what his opponent was saying about him. But who helped you to arrive at this understanding of the opposition tactics?

"I didn't like the folks who were supporting that other fella; I didn't think anything they wanted would be very good for me, so I voted for him."

Of course you didn't like the people who supported the opposition. But who helped you to understand who they were and the ways in which they were supporting the opposition?

The candidate was the major instrument in presenting all these factors which created a favorable reaction. But it was the management of the campaign and the timing of the campaign that caused the voter to see the candidate in such a favorable light. More importantly, this favorable impression was created at about the time when the voter was required to take action, to register his opinion at the polls.

After thirty years in the arena of practical politics—as the manager in command of campaigns, as a specialist advising campaign managers—I can document the following conclusions:

Only a very few successful candidates have any real understanding of why they were victorious.

The segment of the population which is least interested in
politics actually decides the outcome of most elections.

The party organization can help a candidate tremendously,
but it cannot elect him.

Party labels are misleading and party registration is never
the key to a candidate's strength.

Millions of dollars are wasted in every political contest.

Elections are more often lost than won—by that I mean the
errors or mistakes committed by the loser have a more profound
effect upon the outcome than does the positive performance of
the winner.

There is no surer way to lose an election than to think you
have it in the bag.

Virtue in politics is not its own reward. And while the big
issues count, more often than not the little things make the
difference between defeat and victory.

The prevailing notion that a candidate, by his campaign,
must persuade a few more than 50% of the voters to give him
their ballots is a grossly misleading assumption.

Two men were contending for a seat in the U.S. Senate in a
Southern state. They were both good campaigners. They be-
longed to the same party. One candidate, when addressing his
rural audience, would always slip in a statement something like
this: "Now I don't believe in downgrading my opponent—that
ain't the way Americans settle things—but when a man is
seeking to serve his home folks in the U.S. Senate, those folks
are entitled to know all there is to know about him.

"Now, I'm gonna campaign in every county in this state, and
I'm gonna talk on the issues, not on personalities. But I'd be
shirkin' my duty if I didn't tell you that my opponent once
matriculated and that his wife does not deny the fact that she
was once a thespian."

There then followed the usual emotional campaign speech.
When the votes were counted, the loser—with some bitterness—

admitted he had lost the rural vote because the backwoods voters didn't know that matriculation is the act of entering college, that his wife was a "thespian" because she had appeared in amateur theatricals.

In 1958, a Republican incumbent was running for re-election to the U.S. Senate. He was defeated. It is reliably reported that the following campaign tactic contributed materially to that defeat.

The Senator, although no one knew it at the time, was suffering with a brain tumor. Because of this illness, he was subject to dizzy spells. At times he had difficulty in remembering names and carrying a discussion to its logical conclusion.

This situation was seized upon by the opposition as an opportunity to employ the following device:

Six weeks before the general election an attractive man and woman would present themselves at the home of a farmer. Their introduction was routine.

"We're representing the XYZ Opinion Research Poll and we've been sent to ask you some questions if you don't mind."

If the farmer's wife agreed to be interviewed, the callers would produce a typical questionnaire form. They would inquire about the make of tractor used on the farm, the type of implements, the household appliances, etc.

At some point in the interview, when confidence had been established, one or the other of the team would casually remark: "Isn't it too bad about Senator_____?"

If the housewife responded by saying: "What do you mean?", the following explanation would be given:

"About his drinking."

If the housewife defended the Senator, the survey team would explain: "We don't believe the story either, but we were over in another county last week. The Senator was making a political speech and one of the ladies we talked to told us the Senator was too drunk to sit on the platform, that he mumbled when he got up to speak."

The small communities of that state have a strongly religious character. The effect of this tactic was devastating. It was successful because the Senator's management was not prepared to detect and combat this type of assault.

All sorts of people get asked to manage political campaigns. There are almost no professionals in the field. With the exception of the national committees of the parties, there is no full-time employment opportunity. But 43,000 people run for office every two years. Every wise candidate has a manager. There is no school for candidates or for campaign managers. There are thousands of excellent textbooks on political science, but there is very little written about campaign management.

It is my purpose with this book to offer to those seriously interested in political action an understanding of campaign management, campaign techniques and procedures.

My answers to some of the questions raised in this first chapter may be challenged. But there is one promise I can make: the opinions and conclusions presented herein are not theory, they are not arrived at through abstract discussions. Every technique presented can be documented and supported by its use in actual political contests ranging from Massachusetts to Arizona.

I make no apology for my conservative political beliefs. Voters don't elect philosophers to public office, they elect candidates. Approached in the right fashion at the right time, a voter can be persuaded to give his ballot to a candidate whose philosophy is opposed to the cherished notions of the voter.

2 | The Paradox of Elections

Every candidate for elective office is consumed with a desire to win—to be first over the finish line. At the outset of a campaign this desire is frequently concealed by such statements as "I want to serve my country," or "Our viewpoint needs to be represented," or "A great many people for whom I have the deepest respect have asked me to make this race." The candidate may be sincere in his desire to represent a viewpoint or to contribute his special talents in the service of government. But he also wants to win.

Election contests are bitter affairs. The punishment inflicted upon a candidate can be more brutal, more lasting, more destroying than the punches exchanged by prize fighters in the ring. A candidate for minor office in a small constituency will devote at least a month of full time effort to winning the job. Anyone who wants to be elected the governor of a state or to the Congress of the United States will have to spend at least a full year campaigning. Most successful efforts are launched ten to twenty months before the fateful day in November.

In his narrative poem describing a hillbilly fiddlers' contest in Georgia, Stephen Vincent Benet says: "Them that got the mostest claps'd win the bestest prize." The claps for a politician are votes. The procedures for recording the decision are well established. But the serious business of selecting qualified men to serve as temporary rulers of the city, state or nation is frequently referred to as "the side show of politics."

This tremendous expenditure of effort and time and money would seem to require that the aspirant for public office achieve an understanding of how political decisions are reached and just who among his peers will make that final decision.

In every campaign a multiplicity of organizations is enlisted to "get out the vote." "This is the priceless privilege of our free society." "Failure to vote is a denial of responsibility." Service clubs organize campaigns and frequently give out little tags on election day which proclaim: "I voted . . . Have you?" Editorial writers pontificate on the subject. Now and then some revolutionary suggests that if people don't know why they are voting, it would be better for society if they stayed away from the polls.

Political decisions are made by the Indifferent—by that segment of the body politic which really couldn't care less. This is the enormous paradox of democracy—a paradox which has gone almost unnoticed in this nation which prides itself on self-government.

Most managers—indeed, most candidates—are accustomed to the traditional practice of cataloguing their constituents on a basis of economic level, residence, occupation and membership in minority groups. These divisions have some validity. A far more helpful approach and more productive from the standpoint of winning is to classify the voters according to their degree of interest in political matters.

Voting habits or probabilities often reflect the economic level or the affection or disaffection of a minority group. Some political observers believe the rural voter follows one pattern and the urban voter another. The apparent differences charged to these groups is actually a reflection of interest. In all of these accepted subdivisions we find the truly meaningful divisions between the Committed, the Undecided and the Indifferent.

The first classification is by far the most numerous. It embraces all of the voters who are firmly aligned with a particular political philosophy, as well as the more aware among us who view an election as something more than a contest between two attractive personalities. In this Committed group we must include those who are strongly prejudiced toward one party or the other—a condition described in colloquial terms as being a yellow-dog blank—interpreted to mean that a voter would give his ballot to a yellow dog if such were on his party's ticket, in preference to bolting the party.

The Undecideds are frequently those who are truly best informed. They recognize that often times only slight shades of gray separate two candidates. They understand the niceties of the situation. And because in their thinking so many complexities are involved, they frequently find it difficult to reach a decision.

The Indifferents are those who don't vote at all, or vote only in response to an emotional appeal, or as the result of some carefully planned campaign technique which makes it easy for them to reach a decision. The Indifferents decide elections.

During the Truman-Dewey presidential election contest, commencing in June and ending in November, 1948, a research group surveyed a selected sample of the voters in Elmira, New York. The results of this effort were published by the University of Chicago Press in 1954. The authors—Berelson, Lazarsfeld and McPhee—provide evidence to document the argument that it is the Indifferents who decide elections. The descriptive term they use is "the unstable voter."

In that contest 71 per cent of the voters remained constant in their affection for one or the other of the candidates. Thirteen per cent wavered between party and neutral. Sixteen per cent wavered between the parties which, in this instance, must be regarded as shifting back and forth from Dewey to Truman and vice versa.

The authors say: "The people who change most during a campaign are the people who change most between campaigns." At another point. . . . "The resultant fringe of instability surrounding the solid core of more stable American votes arises simply from not caring much one way or the other about the election."

If this construction is correct, we should not be dismayed that sometimes the democratic way of decision seems to elevate the least qualified men to public office. Rather we should be prayerfully thankful democracy works at all, that men of quality and ability are selected by an obviously imperfect system.

When candidate Jones secures the Republican nomination to the United States Senate, he can count on receiving the vote of all the Committeds who give their allegiance to the Republican Party and to the Republican philosophy.

When candidate Smith secures the nomination on the Democrat ticket, he can likewise put down in his column the number of committed registered Democrats in his state.

I do not mean to suggest that a candidate can measure the strength of his party registration and then determine the outcome of the election contest in advance. If this were true, we could do away with elections and declare the winner on the basis of party registration. But the committed vote *is* dependable, it can be determined in advance, and except in those states where there is an overwhelming imbalance between the parties, the committed voters do not have the power of ultimate decisions.

Any study of election day returns over a period of years will demonstrate that in both parties we can find and identify this hard core of immovable voters who cannot be persuaded by any blandishment to desert their party candidates.

It is the continuing ambition of party organizations constantly to enlarge their groups of committed voters. The real health in the democratic process can be found in the fact that neither party has ever been able to enlist and hold a majority of committed support for all of its candidates over any great length of time.

The area of all election contests is limited by a geographical boundary. The smallest unit is the precinct. A number of precincts joined together make up the city or the county or the state. Elections within the states are all determined by the popular vote. In presidential contests, under the present rules in most states,* a candidate who wins a majority of the popular vote within the state receives all of that state's electoral votes. Students of our election practices from other countries are frequently dismayed when they discover that although Franklin Roosevelt was elected President of the United States four times, the people did not vote directly for Roosevelt—giving their ballots instead to electors who were pledged to vote for Roosevelt.

The number of committed voters in any precinct or in all the precincts of a constituency can readily be determined. This process of identification is simple but only a few candidates and campaign managers recognize the value of making such a determination.

A review of voting history in the precinct will reveal that the poorest Republican candidate has historically received a certain number of votes or a certain percentage of the total votes cast. The term "poor" is used here not as a judgment on the candidate's qualifications but at an indication of his showing in the contest. The number of votes cast for the poorest Democrat candidate added to the number of votes given to the poorest Republican candidate will reveal the probable total of committed votes in that precinct.

This reconstruction of voting habits will be of no value in a

---

* *A few states have freed their electoral college delegates from commitment to any Presidential candidate on the ballot.*

one-party state where the outcome is determined in the primaries. But in a state which has selected its leaders from both parties in recent years, an analysis of prior election returns will prove to be of significant value.

If, from the standpoint of the votes received, the most unsuccessful Republican candidate has enjoyed thirty per cent of the total votes cast, and the most unsuccessful Democrat candidate has enjoyed forty per cent of the total votes cast, the astute campaign manager will recognize that since the committed voters amount to seventy per cent of the state's total, the remaining thirty per cent hold the power of decision.

In making such an analysis it is important to study at least the three most recent elections. Figures should not be compiled entirely on the outcome of the races for the top offices—that is, for governor and for the Congress.

That segment of the thirty per cent who are truly *undecided* will probably reach their own conclusions independently. It is their full understanding of the points at issue which contributes to their indecision. They are acutely aware of their responsibility and will probably not be greatly influenced by the campaign devices designed to reach the indifferent group. The undecided almost always vote, but the indifferent voter must be prodded into action or he very likely won't vote at all.

The candidate whose party's nominees have historically enjoyed a smaller number of committed votes must make a greater effort to win. But, essentially, the task confronting both candidates and both managers is the same—to reach the thirty to thirty-five per cent of the voters, undecided and indifferent, who when their votes are added to the committed votes, will give one candidate or the other a majority.

By this analysis the target area comes into sharp focus. The two candidates are not competing for the approval of all the voters or for the approval of 50.01 per cent of the committed voters. Their task is to reach enough of the undecided and uncommitted or indifferent voters to bring their total to 50.01

per cent. Thus, the Republican, who has at the start a committed vote amounting to thirty per cent of the historic total, must persuade a few more than twenty per cent of the remaining voters to place their stamp of approval upon his candidacy.

Most analysts agree that in the presidential contest of 1960, candidate Kennedy was tremendously benefited by the Catholic issue.

From a truly objective viewpoint, it makes little difference whether the man in the White House is a Protestant or a Roman Catholic. It is to be hoped that any aspirant for such high office will be guided by deep religious conviction. But the Kennedy campaign exploited the opportunity to emphasize the Catholic issue out of all true proportion.

During the campaign the candidate stressed his identification with the Roman Catholic Church. In his speeches and in the public statements of his supporters, there was the undisguised suggestion that to vote against Kennedy was an act of bigotry, the protest of a voter moving not from logic but from passion.

It is probable that a substantial number of the indifferent voters gave their ballots to Mr. Nixon because of prejudice. But the Kennedy campaign which faced the issue in the early days of that effort made it difficult, if not impossible, for the Nixon supporters to ask the Indifferents to vote against Kennedy *because* of his Roman Catholic religion.

Political campaigns generate and fatten on a certain type of hysteria. Campaign speeches frequently feature appeals based upon emotion rather than upon logic and reason. The voter is harrassed by a host of candidates seeking his support. In contests where it is sometimes difficult to find a truly major difference between competing candidates, the voter is almost forced to rest his decision upon some relatively unimportant difference.

The experienced campaign manager will devise his strategy to sharpen the differences between his candidate and the opponent. These differences may have no real bearing upon the candidate's competence. But if they can be displayed in such a fashion as to be easily recognizable, the Indifferents will show their gratitude for this assistance by voting. And if the manager has been successful, if the differences reflect credit to his candidate and imply discredit to the opposition, the Indifferents will vote for his candidate.

The indifferent voter—the voter who is not solidly and completely committed philosophically or emotionally to one or the other of the two major parties—is representative of those who fail to vote.

We can boast that approximately sixty-three per cent of the qualified population participated in the 1960 presidential contest. But we must not lose sight of the fact that almost thirty-seven per cent of the free American citizenry regarded that election as so unimportant as not to demand their attendance at the polling places. These stay-at-homes frequently contribute vitally to the outcome of an election.

In 1936 Franklin D. Roosevelt received a total vote of 27,751,597.* His Republican opponent, Alfred Landon, earned 16,679,583 votes. In 1940 F.D.R., running for a third term, was given 27,243,466 votes. In the same year 22,304,755 citizens marked their ballots for the Republican, Wendell Willkie. The remarkable fact here is not that Willkie received more than 5,600,000 votes over Landon. The significant figure is that 5,117,041 more votes were cast. A portion of this increase can, of course, be attributed to new voters; but most of these ballots were cast by voters who had stayed away from the polls in 1936.

In the 1960 presidential contest we find some startling examples of what failure to vote can mean to the outcome of an election. Approximately 59,000 citizens in the State of Illinois marked their ballots for a congressional candidate but failed

* *Voting statistics used in this paragraph are taken from the 1964 Edition of* The World Almanac.

to indicate a preference for one or the other of the presidential candidates. Mr. Kennedy won Illinois by some 9,000 votes.

A majority of these 59,000 voters gave their support to a Republican candidate for the House or Senate. They simply refused to vote for Mr. Nixon or for Mr. Kennedy.

Students of the outcome in Illinois believe this failure to express a preference in the presidential contest must be attributed to the influence of those who were urging Republicans to disavow Mr. Nixon. This objection was based upon a belief that Mr. Nixon was not sufficiently conservative. It is quite fair to state that those who refused to vote for a presidential candidate in Illinois contributed materially to Mr. Kennedy's victory.

The indifferent voter can be reached and motivated by a variety of techniques. In 1952 Barry Goldwater, a Republican candidate for the United States Senate in Arizona, appeared certain to be defeated. Goldwater was challenging a two-term experienced Democrat politician, Ernest McFarland, who was then serving as Majority Leader in the United States Senate. From this position of incumbency and party leadership, McFarland appeared unbeatable.

The party registration in Arizona favored the Democrats by about five to one. It was obvious Goldwater could not win on the committed Republican strength. Many responsible leaders in the Democrat camp regarded Goldwater's challenge as an annoyance not to be taken seriously. In support of their position they relied on the fact that it would be necessary to persuade at least twenty-five per cent of the registered Democrats to cross the party line.

In planning this campaign we started with a detailed precinct analysis. This told us it was possible for Goldwater to win.

Arizona had elected a Republican governor in 1950. In that campaign the Republican candidate was Howard Pyle—a radio broadcaster who had for years conducted a rather sentimental program reading poetry on behalf of a mortuary parlor. Pyle's voice and Pyle's name were known to almost every citizen in Arizona. But he had no political experience, no demonstrated competence in public administration.

The Democrat nominee was Mrs. Anna Frohmiller, an extremely capable individual. She had served 16 years as state auditor. During her administration she had established a magnificent reputation as an effective, efficient administrator. It can be argued that she would have made a better governor as a result of this vast experience.

Pyle, the Republican, was elected. The Democrats dismissed this upset as being based on masculine prejudice against having a woman as chief executive.

Women have been elected to the office of governor in other states. If Anna Frohmiller was competent to be elected and re-elected as state auditor—a responsible position—she was, on the basis of competence and qualification, eligible to serve as governor of Arizona.

There is no way of determining exactly why Pyle won. His victory demonstrated there were not enough committed Democrat voters in Arizona to determine the outcome of any election. Surely any citizen who would make his decision on the basis of the sex of the candidate has no strong commitment to party or philosophy. Such action is the result of prejudice rather than reason. And if these people had moved across the party line once, it was a fair assumption that they could be persuaded to do it twice.

Our study of that 1950 election convinced us that Goldwater could be elected to the United States Senate as a Republican, provided we could reach and persuade a sufficient number of the Indifferents. It is true these voters we needed were registered in the opposite party. But they had crossed the party line in 1950 for a relatively superficial reason. It was our job to persuade them to cross the party line in 1952.

We had reason to believe the overwhelming Democrat Party registration was not in any sense a reflection of solid commitment to that political faith. When Arizona became a state in 1912 the population had a distinct Southern character. In the first four elections a Democrat had been elected governor. In all the years between 1912 and 1952 only three Republicans had been elected to the state's highest office, and only one Republican has been elected to the United States Senate—and that one in the Harding landslide of 1920. During the intervening years most newcomers were advised by friends and business associates to register in the Democrat Party for the very compelling reason that the Republican weakness actually made the Democrat primary the only real contest. Candidates chosen in the Democrat Party primary waltzed through the general election. If a citizen in Arizona wanted to participate in the selection of his local public officials, his only chance to voice a preference was in the Democrat primary. But Arizona had voted for Coolidge in 1924 and for Hoover in 1928 when the percentage of Democrat registration was much higher than the five to one which confronted us in 1952.

The odds were all against a Goldwater victory. We conceded this. Arizona voters were in the habit of electing a Democrat to the United States Senate. To win it would be necessary to persuade ninety per cent of the registered Republicans to vote for Goldwater. This would require effective party action on Election Day. Then, because of the imbalance in registration, we had to persuade at least one of every four Democrats to cross his party line and vote for a Republican candidate. Actually we planned two campaigns—one to reach and inspire the Republicans. Above everything else we must persuade them victory was possible. The second phase of our campaign was aimed squarely at the Indifferents and the Undecideds in the Democrat ranks.

Goldwater was a tiger on the campaign trail. He appeared before Republican-sponsored audiences in every community in the state. But in our television, radio, newspaper and direct mail efforts our appeal was aimed at the nominal Democrats.

In Arizona lists of registered voters by party declaration are available. These lists are divided into precincts, making it possible to plan selected mailings.

One of the devices we used clearly supports the contention that the indifferent voter can be persuaded to reach a decision by a device or technique which rests not at all on the qualifications or philosophy of the candidate.

We purchased over fifty thousand ordinary government-printed post cards. We had these addressed by hand to be mailed to registered Democrats. The message was also handwritten—addressed to the voter by first name.

"Dear Jim, . . . Tuesday is Election Day. I sure hope you'll vote and I hope you will vote for me. Barry."

What a ridiculous, futile exercise! Anyone receiving such a card should know immediately that the candidate could not possibly have taken the time to write the message personally.

Individuals receiving the post cards who didn't know the candidate might very well be offended by the use of the first name. And the message—so obvious, so banal, so undistinguished—"Tuesday is Election Day"—the recipient would have to be dead or in solitary confinement not to know that Tuesday was election day.

"I sure hope that you'll vote." Well, all candidates hope people will vote. The newspapers and the radio and television had been urging and imploring the people to vote.

"I hope you will vote for me." Every candidate hopes the voter will approve his candidacy.

"You're wasting the money," I was told by a member of the old guard Republican leadership in Arizona, "if you think 50,000 or 60,000 people are going to be moved to vote for Goldwater by that post card." "That isn't what I think at all," I replied. We mailed the cards so they would be received on Saturday or Monday preceding election day.

I knew that most of the voters receiving that post card appeal couldn't be moved to cross the party line by a plea from their mother. But I also knew that if I were lucky, perhaps ten per cent of the cards would be received by the Indifferents, by those who had not yet made up their minds, by voters who were not committed emotionally or ideologically to the Democrat candidate.

I was convinced that a personal communication, a post card without any political slogan, just a request for a vote, made on a first-name basis, might be enough of a reason to secure their support.

There was no way to determine accurately the total impact of this post card solicitation. We did get a representative feedback. Our poll watchers reported that in the precincts solicited a number of voters showed up with the post cards in their hands or in their pockets.

After the election, when I was trying to determine why people had voted for Goldwater, the post card was mentioned frequently. Any number of people told us they knew the busy candidate didn't have time to write the post card, but they were pleased to have the request and they responded.

If this device gained even one thousand votes which might otherwise have gone to the Democrat McFarland, it was responsible for two thousand of the seven thousand vote margin by which Goldwater won that election.

I have been privileged to play some role in seventeen different campaigns for the United States Senate. In twelve of these the first step in campaign planning has been to identify the Indifferents. The second step is to devise ways and means of reaching this group with an appeal which can be accepted as a reason for their favorable action on election day.

In 1962 there was a necessary special election for a seat in Congress in the district surrounding San Antonio, Texas. Many factors contributed to the ultimate outcome. The Democrat candidate was Henry Gonzalez, a liberal Democrat of Mexican ancestry, who had previously been elected to the Texas Legislature. His Republican opponent, a bright and attractive candidate, articulated the conservative philosophy.

Texas is a Democrat state. But this district had given a substantial vote to Richard Nixon. John Tower had won there in 1961 as a candidate for the United States Senate.

In the final two weeks the then Vice President of the United States, Lyndon Johnson, entered the district and campaigned vigorously. The burden of the argument offered by the Gonzalez supporters in those final days was this: "We hope you're not going to vote against Henry just because he's a Mexican and a Roman Catholic." Gonzalez won.

Of course no thoughtful voter would permit the fact that Gonzalez was of Mexican origin and a Roman Catholic to decide his vote. But the indifferent voter who is not deeply committed will frequently respond to the careful development of a difference between candidates which has no valid bearing upon their competence.

The numerical strength of the Indifferents is not sufficient to permit them to make the political decision independent of a committed group. Perhaps my years in the political wars have prejudiced my judgment, but it is impossible for me to argue against the proposition that in almost every election superficial considerations influence a sufficient number of the citizen voters to determine the outcome. More often than not political decisions are made by those who respond to a carefully thought out strategy, who act more from emotion than reason, who are the least passionate in their political conviction, who couldn't care less.

3 | The Campaign Manager

Success in a political contest can be attributed to the personality of the candidate, the vigor and strength of the party organization, or to a domestic or international situation which comes to crisis at a fortuitous time.

The great depression defeated Herbert Hoover. The imminence of World War II elected Franklin Roosevelt to a third term. But these external forces are the exception rather than the rule.

Men have been elected on sheer personality or, as in the case of candidate Eisenhower, as the result of popularity earned in a field apart from politics. But the majority of political contests are won by attractive candidates who conduct skillful, well-timed campaigns.

In baseball the same man cannot be both pitcher and catcher. In politics the candidate cannot successfully manage his own campaign—a truism which was painfully demonstrated when I attempted to manage my own campaign for the Republican nomination for the United States Senate in 1962.

The candidate is on public display twenty-four hours a day. He must keep a schedule of appointments and appearances. He must shake hands with the voters and never appear to be hurried. He must be competent and compelling on television. His

25

speeches must be addressed to subjects which concern the audience and to be effective they must be meaningful.

It is the job of the campaign manager to make the candidate look good, to map the strategy, to command the supporting troops. To do these things successfully, he must enjoy the full confidence and trust of the candidate, and he must be given authority to make all decisions.

Candidates rate the headlines. Campaign managers are shielded from public attention by the shadow of the candidate. This is as it should be. The manager must retain a perspective and objectivity which is denied to the central figures on the political stage.

A proper campaign organization will enlist the special skills and the talents of many people. The manager must direct and inspire. His job is to build an efficient, effective group of specialists who can produce under the teriffic pressure and tension of political battle. Unless there is a clear line of authority, the result is likely to be only so much organized wheel spinning.

It is not always easy to find men experienced in the art of running campaigns. In this field there is no substitute for on-the-job training. There are no college courses, no textbooks that deal exclusively with the peculiar, distinctive and usually brutal task of winning an election.

The purpose of this book is to make winning elections easier —not to complicate the process. The ideal campaign manager probably hasn't been born. But a job description will give some idea of the enormity of the problem and at the same time suggest the qualities a manager should possess. Every candidate wrestles with the problem of "What kind of a person should I select as manager?"

The manager must know the constituency—its geography, its people, its commercial interests and those special sectional rivalries that frequently complicate a statewide political contest.

The manager should have some acquaintance with the media

that will be employed in the campaign . . . television, radio, newspaper, direct mail. Since no single individual is likely to possess great competence in all of these fields, the problem becomes one of finding a manager who can enlist the right talents for these specialized activities.

The manager should have a strong interest in politics. A technician skilled in the mechanics can perform satisfactorily under almost any situation. But that final extra effort which may make the difference between victory or defeat is more likely to be forthcoming if the manager and the candidate share a common political conviction.

The manager must be able to get along well with people, to control the overly ambitious and to be able to resist the pressures which build up when human egos clash.

The manager must be able to say "no" without giving offense; to say "yes" and stick to it. Frequently he must say "no" to the candidate. And when he makes a commitment it must be kept.

In this regard candidates have much more latitude. They can, by innuendo or suggestion, imply a promise for future delivery. When the manager says something will be done, it must be done—and before the day of election which ends that campaign.

The campaign manager must be cold-blooded and hard-nosed about spending campaign funds. In every political contest there are literally hundreds of people who come forward with a sure-fire scheme to bring victory. If only—if only the candidate advertises in their particular program, sponsors their barbecue, gives financial support to a project being urged by a minority group.

Party leaders will put pressure on the manager to favor their choice for a campaign itinerary. Important supporters will insist the candidate spend what may be an unnecessary amount of time in their bailiwick. And to all these pressures and requests the manager must find a diplomatic refusal.

In addition to all these things, the manager must understand how the voter is motivated to reach a decision and be able to devise an over-all strategy which will increase the popularity of his candidate.

I have known lawyers, newsmen, business executives and advertising men who have made excellent campaign managers— not because of who they were but *what* they were—intelligent, informed, endowed with administrative ability and committed to the cause they served.

In my own experience each campaign has been slightly different from the rest, just as each candidate differs from his contemporaries. But the objective in all was the same—to win. The problems are similar and the solutions which have been effective in one campaign have also been effective in others.

No one of my acquaintance has ever set out to make a career of managing political campaigns. The work is spasmodic. At best it offers employment for a few months every two, four or six years. The wages paid are never enough to compensate for the labor involved. In my first senatorial campaign I earned $1,800. In the second one, which required more than six months of concentrated effort, I was paid $3,500. But there are other compensations. Politics deal with the destiny of our society, shape the world of tomorrow in which our children must live, and each campaign becomes a unique experience.

Lawyers who manage campaigns make valuable contacts in the political world. Corporate clients who must deal with the government are anxious to be represented by a lawyer who can claim close relationship with powerful political figures. During the conduct of the campaign the lawyer manager acquires a knowledge of his constituency which can be put to beneficial use for present and future clients.

Newspaper men and writers often follow their candidate after election to serve as administrative assistants, press secretaries, etc. Many of the young men who now work on Capitol Hill in the office of a congressman or a senator moved into these important positions after helping win an election.

Managing someone else's campaign is frequently the stepping-stone to becoming a successful candidate and most managers have a more than passing interest in a public life. Then, there is the excitement. A fierce campaign for public office generates an atmosphere of competition not to be equalled in any other endeavor.

For the serious student of politics, managing a campaign provides greater insight and better understanding than can ever be acquired in a classroom. Professor Conrad Joyner, who teaches government at the University of Arizona and recently produced an excellent book entitled *The Republican Dilemma,* acquired his special insight while working on the campaign trail for Governor Mark Hatfield of Oregon. Joyner's counterparts can be found on many college campuses.

I have been privileged to travel more than 100,000 miles on political missions. I have been thrust into almost daily association with the public men of my time. My world has been enlarged with friendships in more than a dozen states. And the political idiosyncracies of these areas are now my secrets. Every candidate I have served has given me a new insight, a new understanding of the art and practice of politics.

In 1950, United States Senator Carl Hayden (D-Ariz.) was challenged by a vigorous, well financed opponent. We had good reason to believe that this candidate had been put in the race by two special interest groups, anxious to pressure Hayden into supporting some legislation they desired. Halfway through the campaign a spokesman for the sponsors of our opponent tried without success to make an appointment with Hayden to discuss a "mutual problem."

When the campaign was over and Hayden had won the primary, we met by prearrangement on the Wednesday after Election Day to have a victory drink in the Kiva Club—a swank rendezvous located on top of the Hotel Westward Ho in Phoenix.

The Hayden campaign had marked my first participation in a United States Senate contest. I was greatly pleased at Hayden's victory. The world was ours. The voters had just said so.

In this happy frame of mind I casually asked the Senator what he had been doing that Wednesday. His reply is still vivid in my memory:

"Why, I was downtown so I went into such-and-such an office building and paid my respects to Mr. So-and-so. Then I wandered over to such-and-such an address and said 'hello' to Mr. So-and-so."

Hayden had named the two men who had sponsored his opponent in the primary. My reaction of incredulous astonishment caused the senator to grin with wry appreciation.

"Let me tell you something, Steve," he said, "never give your enemies any more reason than they already have to go on hating you."

In this competitive world, where men and ideas constantly clash, I have never been given better advice.

Most of the opinions expressed in this book are the result of my experience as manager and consultant to managers of campaigns for the United States Senate. I shall attempt in every instance to offer specific examples of success in support of those conditions or techniques I advance. It well may be that some of my candidates would have been elected without the use of these devices, but out of all the prescriptions for victory offered here there is one I regard as paramount—the manager must command the campaign effort. Any division of authority between the manager and the candidate or betweeen the manager and his assistants will, at some point in the campaign, produce disaster.

I argue this not because I think the campaign manager is in every case or in any case more competent than the candidate. The campaign must have unity. The campaign must move steadily forward from its starting position to its objective of victory. Any delay or deviation from the basic strategic plan will waste precious time and money.

The manager can be objective; the candidate cannot completely divorce himself from the emotional stress of being the candidate.

The manager who has selected the strategy, after consultation with the candidate and his crew of experts, must be in a position of authority to implement that strategy.

In my own experience I have found that good candidates are quite willing to delegate the proper authority. In the 1960 campaigns Senator Curtis told his working staff in Nebraska that he wanted me to review every piece of literature and approve every step proposed to advance the campaign.

In Colorado, United States Senator Gordon Allott's managers accepted every suggestion without question. When I asked Chuck Colson how things were going in Massachusetts (Colson was the active manager for Senator Leverett Saltonstall) he said, "We're running it by the book," referring to the original campaign outline upon which this more detailed work is based.

I suffered through my first political experience more than thirty years ago. An immensely popular political figure, who was then the elected Secretary of State in Arizona, decided to enter the primary and seek the gubernatorial nomination. His supporters wanted to publish a campaign newspaper. This was in the depths of the depression and when they offered me $50 a week to edit their propaganda, I accepted promptly.

Our candidate's two opponents were relatively unknown politically. Our man was backed strongly by the mining and railroad interests in Arizona. We had a handsome campaign budget. At the outset victory seemed inevitable.

As the campaign progressed, confusion increased. There was no unity, there was no theme. Our man, like Don Quixote, went around the state tilting at windmills. But for all of this he was still in the lead the night before primary election day.

The Democrat Party in those days held a final climactic public meeting in the largest outdoor arena in the state. More than 10,000 people gathered to hear the candidates make their final appeals. In addition to the three men running for governor, there were ten or fifteen candidates for lesser offices included on the program.

Our man spoke first. He had refused to prepare a written text; he was the old, experienced campaigner, proud of an ability to deliver stirring oratory extemporaneously. He did. He talked for one hour and eighteen minutes. He alienated the affection of every Democrat in that stadium. Supporters of other candidates resented his usurping all the time. His own supporters were bored. His two opponents spoke for less than ten minutes each.

I watched the agony on the campaign manager's face. He knew and I knew we had lost the election. Our man ran third. If there had been five candidates, he would have been fifth. And he lost through an unbridled display of that ego which is standard equipment with most candidates.

A poor campaign manager is almost certain to lose the campaign regardless of the candidate's qualifications, but even a poor manager who has the authority to act is better than no manager at all. In my experience I witnessed only one campaign which operated without a manager and was successful. This candidate won because of his own personal popularity and the weakness of his opponent, who had been involved in a scandal.

My first opportunity to exercise full command of a campaign came in 1942 when a longtime friend, Ernest Roach, asked me to manage his effort to become sheriff of Maricopa County, Arizona. Our budget was less than $4,000. We estimated that our opponent spent $25,000. Roach was not a colorful candidate. His opponent had been a world champion cowboy, was extremely popular—endowed with an outgoing personality that made friends easily.

We had just one great asset. Roach, a veteran law enforcement officer, had a record of experience which made him, by all odds, the best qualified man for the job.

It was in this campaign that I first used the Burma Shave type jingle political signs. With $4,000 to spend and the fifth largest county in the nation to cover, a campaign manager has to be cost conscious. We borrowed some steel fence posts from a friendly rancher. We bought some inexpensive pine lumber, 1″ x 8″ x 6′. We had the signs stenciled on a kind of oil cloth which is inexpensive and durable. We tacked and glued the signs to the pine boards and attached these by bolts to the steel fence posts.

In the West, at least, Burma Shave signs have produced many smiles for the traveling motorist. The jingles are impudent and to the point. There were five lines to our sign. We put them on all the county roads, spaced about 150 feet apart for easy reading. This was the jingle:

> "Ain't no cowhand . . .
> Nor politician . . .
> But when crooks pop up . . .
> He's in there pitchin' . . .
> Roach for Sheriff!"

A second jingle read:

> "Fourteen years a deputy . . .
> Trained by the F.B.I. . . .
> His record shows to you and me . . .
> For Sheriff he's the guy . . .
> Roach for Sheriff!"

Our total cost for 120 sets of these jingle signs was less than $200. No one had ever used this kind of approach in local politics before. Roach was elected.

As the result of this experience with Roach and with his successor in office, I acquired enough confidence to insist that the manager of a campaign be given authority to run the campaign.

In this key relationship of any political campaign, when the candidate agrees to accept the ruling of the manager, it is equally important for the manager to recognize that he is not the candidate. The manager who takes to the hustings with the candidate, who makes all the appearances, who is as much on the go as the candidate himself, really isn't a manager at all. He's nothing more than a functioning political valet. The effective manager, like the man in charge of a good baseball team, must call the plays and let someone else run the bases.

The manager-candidate relationship should be one of mutual trust and divided responsibility. It is not the manager's job to think for the candidate or to manipulate him like a puppet on a string. What the manager must do is help the candidate to express his ideas, to display his true personality and to avoid mistakes. The manager should have time to think; the candidate has precious little time for anything. The manager who shares his candidate's conviction and political faith will coordinate all of the activities of the entire campaign staff into an effective team effort with the special skills of each member adding strength to the candidate's image.

This is a delicate and precious relationship—one that is not often achieved, but one well worth striving for.

Money is necessary for political victory. Before an organization can be built or strategy developed the candidate and the manager must adopt a tentative budget, name a campaign treasurer and a campaign finance chairman. The treasurer will handle the funds raised, pay the bills and keep the records. The finance chairman should be free to devote all his efforts to fund raising.

A simple and effective method of safeguarding campaign funds is to require a purchase order signed by the manager for every campaign expenditure. This will not be as complicated or as tedious as it might appear. If an advertising agency is employed, the amount of money allocated to the various media can be transferred to the agency on a single purchase order. But unless one individual has the authority—and the sole authority—to authorize expenditures, the campaign funds will melt away.

The size of the paid campaign staff will depend upon the amount of money available. In the first Goldwater campaign I had one secretary, a volunteer publicity man, two college students who erected the Burma Shave jingle signs and a commercial artist. In that campaign we did not use an agency. The artist made the newspaper layouts and prepared the literature for printing. We wrote all the copy—speeches, radio, television, newspapers and pamphlets.

An advisory group of knowledgeable experts should be assembled early in the campaign and consulted constantly throughout the campaign. A group cannot write a speech, prepare an ad or decide on the copy for TV and radio, but the campaign which does not have available an advisory group will be seriously limited. The members of the group should be chosen for their loyalty to the candidate, for their experience in other campaigns, for their competence in a particular field or medium and for their acquaintance with the political idiosyncracies of the constituency.

Such a group will probably include one or two lawyers who have been interested in politics, a newspaper writer or editor, one or two experienced party officials who are not at the moment accountable to the regular party machinery.

Both the manager and the candidate need this kind of sounding board—a place where ideas and suggestions can be brainstormed—and it is always helpful to have the critical opinion of a cynical, experienced professional politician.

The campaign manager must prepare a timetable, keeping in mind that constant acceleration is essential. The schedule or itinerary should be placed in the hands of a gracious, efficient secretary who will keep track of requests, make up the candidate's calendar and be responsible for all the details which contribute to the success of the candidate's personal appearances.

When the image and the theme of the campaign have been developed, as suggested in the chapter on *Image,* the manager will keep the campaign on course, stubbornly refusing to permit any deviation.

If the Cell Groups are to be organized, this is the responsibility of the manager. If the Foot Soldier program is selected, the manager will select someone to take charge of this important and vote-producing activity.

The manager need not create all the advertising copy, the television scripts and the candidate's speeches, but he should select the subjects to be covered. Only in this way can he maintain control of the campaign emphasis.

The manager must be ready to encourage the candidate when that is needed, and he must prevent the candidate from making mistakes.

From a tactical viewpoint, campaigns are more often lost than won. By that I mean the errors of the opposition offer your candidate the best possibility for victory. The campaign manager must recognize every blind alley issue and keep the campaign from falling into these pitfalls. A blind alley issue is some small matter of controversy which does not bear directly on the central concerns of the constituency. At the same time the manager must find ways to lead the opposition into a blind alley.

In 1958 Goldwater formally opened his campaign for reelection in a radio speech delivered from Prescott, the Senator's sentimental point of origin. In that speech Goldwater bitterly condemned his opponent for having voted in favor of a particular piece of legislation when his opponent was a member of the United States Senate.

In developing this speech we had relied upon the research staff of the Republican Senatorial Campaign Committee. Unfortunately, the researcher hadn't gone far enough. This particular vote was one of those peculiar parliamentary things which occur in the Senate where a vote of *aye* on the immediate motion was actually a negative vote on the full proposition offered. Goldwater's opponent promptly cried "foul" and then produced the proof of our error.

Members of the Goldwater advisory team agreed the Senator should apologize. I vehemently disagreed. "If we do this," I argued, "it will keep the issue alive. If we say nothing, it will die. If we apologize and admit that we were completely wrong, our opponent can attack everything we say from here on in. I can hear him now: 'Senator Goldwater claims so-and-so is the truth. I wonder if he is any more certain of this than when he was finally forced to apologize for his untruth about my voting record.' "

I could visualize the campaign swinging away from the major issues and concentrating on this one mistake. Our opponent had made his point. If we did not respond, either to confirm or deny, there was little more he could say.

We didn't apologize and we won.

The good campaign manager will suffer in every adversity experienced by his candidate. There will come days when he questions his own judgment. Having full authority carries the penalty of being responsible for the errors as well as for the successes.

When the campaign is over, when your candidate wins, he and he alone will enjoy the spotlight. The manager and the campaign staff must be prepared to be ignored in victory.

4 | The Image of a Candidate

Image is a Madison Avenue term with a not altogether whole-some connotation. It suggests a fabricated picture, an arti-ficially contrived impression produced by the creative skills of the advertising man, a composite, carefully nurtured profile designed to create a favorable impression upon the beholder.

The image of the candidate is the public appreciation of the candidate's personality, philosophy, intelligence, competence and performance record. The image is what the public sees, what the public knows, what the public believes about the man or the woman who is soliciting their approval at the ballot box.

In a political campaign the problem of image does not call for fabrication or contrivance or distortion. The voters will always penetrate even the smallest deception. A candidate may win one election by pretending to be something he is not, but when the next judgment day rolls around the voters will express their anger against the deceiver and against themselves for having been deceived.

The problem of image for the candidate and the campaign manager calls for the wise and considered use of emphasis.

Public figures all labor under a common delusion. They vastly over-estimate the impact of their own publicity. Politicians,

39

like the stars in the theatrical world, feed their egos by reading
every word said about them, by listening eagerly to every spoken
comment. The business of government absorbs their undivided
attention. In a very real sense they live in a world apart from the
society they seek to serve. Because of their consuming interest
in the affairs of government and in the actions and statements of
other politicians, they believe without question that all their
fellow citizens have this same passionate concern for the affairs
of government.

At the outset of any campaign—when the candidate and the
manager and the staff, either paid or volunteer, are gathered
together for the first planning session—this question must be
answered:

"Who is this candidate we are asking the voters to support?"

The traditional politician who has won election to public
office will dismiss this inquiry as a frivolous waste of time. The
professionals who have enjoyed a long association with the
candidate will likely agree that everyone knows their "stalwart
champion of morality, wisdom and political leadership."

The reaction to this question which I asked so many times in
1959 and 1960 demonstrates the monumental lack of objectivity
which contributes to the common errors of most political campaigns.

United States Senator Carl Curtis from Nebraska is a knowledgeable, intelligent, effective politician. Curtis is a likeable man
with a strict, no nonsense attitude. In eighteen months of close
association he earned my admiration and my affection.

As the first act of that Nebraska campaign Senator Curtis assembled ten or twelve of his close political advisers at a meeting
in the Cornhusker Hotel in Lincoln, Nebraska. Dick Spelts,
who had been chosen by Curtis to manage the state-wide campaign, is a successful lumberman in Grand Island. Dick Herman,
who, with his brother, operates Herman Brothers Trucking
Company in Omaha, is a brilliant, young executive who brought
considerable political experience to his assignment as leader of

the Curtis forces in populous Douglas County. Herman and Spelts carried the major Curtis burden in that campaign. But when we met in the Cornhusker Hotel both Herman and Spelts completely missed the point of my initial question: "Who is Carl Curtis?"

To them Carl Curtis was an effective congressman, the winner of a very difficult campaign for the United States Senate, a champion of conservative Republican doctrine, an effective member of the McClellan Labor Rackets Committee. They construed my question as a personal request for background information arising from the fact that I was not a resident of Nebraska.

I wasn't at all interested in the description of the Carl Curtis they knew and admired. In a real sense, my question wasn't addressed to them at all. The answer I sought was: "What is the public image of Carl Curtis? How do the people of Nebraska regard Carl Curtis?" When this was explained, the Senator promptly understood the reason for the question and agreed that we should take steps necessary to find the answer.

If the people who are closest to the candidate don't know who he is, who does? Why, the constituency, of course. And only by combining the opinions of a representative group of voters is it possible to determine the true image a candidate brings to a campaign.

Those who are equipped through long acquaintance to know the candidate best can make a contribution to this determination. A practical procedure is to ask everyone on the campaign staff to answer a simple questionnaire. This same information should be solicited from those who have great interest in politics—editors of newspapers, political writers, party officials.

As a part of this process it is necessary to list all the qualities or positions which can be regarded as the assets your candidate brings to the campaign. A comparable list of liabilities must be made.

To determine what the average attitude of the constituency is toward your candidate, it will be extremely useful to distribute questionnaires to a wide segment of the voting population. This can be accomplished in many ways. In the Mid-Western states county and state fairs are great gathering places. Most political parties maintain booths at these fairs, and the citizen is always flattered when his opinion is solicited. From such an inquiry the campaign manager will acquire some startling facts.

In 1959 at the start of the Nebraska campaign we used a questionnaire to determine the public's knowledge of United States Senator Carl Curtis. More than thirty per cent of those who responded said they had never seen or heard of U.S. Senator Carl Curtis. (The type of questionnaires used will be explained fully in the chapter on polling.)

Impossible! Incredible! There must be something wrong with the figures! Some practical joker had pulled a funny!

No, indeed. The figures were accurate and in some states where the urban population is greater, where in-and-out migration is responsible for a perpetually unstable electorate, the percentage will be even higher. Keep in mind that, even in the hotly contested presidential race, less than seventy per cent of those citizens qualified to vote will actually go to the polls.

This kind of "How well do they know me" survey is an effective antidote for the candidate who believes his personality and activities are recognized by every voter in the constituency.

Of course the purpose of the image survey goes far beyond this determination of how well your candidate is known. If properly conducted, it will give you a true reflection of how the voters see your candidate and, more importantly, will permit the staff to identify the candidate's liabilities. Once the true image of the candidate is determined, the full emphasis of the campaign can be devoted to stressing the candidate's assets and to minimizing his liabilities.

Assume for a moment that your candidate shows up as a man of great experience in government but a poor public speaker, one whose formal addresses either lack color or are too long or fail because of the candidate's manner of delivery. It may develop that your candidate is very good in the familiar question and answer aspect of political meetings. The campaign manager will immediately schedule fewer and shorter formal addresses and place the emphasis on the question and answer phase.

In the 1960 presidential campaign Richard Nixon's experience in government was a recognized asset. Even those who voted against him readily conceded that Nixon's training as Vice President had equipped him to handle the job as Chief Executive. Nixon's appearance was a liability. The television camera was particularly unkind to Nixon's face and general appearance.

Kennedy, a relatively unknown Senator from Massachusetts, photographed well and projected great charm. Now, certainly, we should not choose our presidents on the basis of appearance or charm; but, unfortunately, this is the deciding factor in the minds of many voters. It was a gross error to permit the voters to view Kennedy and Nixon side by side. Nixon, the logical, forceful speaker, would have done extremely well on radio. Had his managers emphasized the solid, homely appearance of Nixon, had they prevented him from appearing in competition with the matinee idol exterior of Kennedy, the results might have been quite different.

Some candidates, when interviewed by the press, are simply incapable of giving a direct answer to a direct question. They always insist upon making a speech and cloaking their opinions in grand eloquent language which is impossible to quote and, if quoted, carries a suggestion of insincerity. Other candidates are all too eager to respond with a quick, glib answer. If your candidate has a tendency to "pop off," to give an opinion which is not based on real understanding, the wise manager will minimize the opportunity for such interviews.

In the 1960 South Dakota campaign the voters recognized U.S. Senator Karl Mundt as a tough-minded fighter. Mundt is naturally a soft-spoken, courteous gentleman who devastates his enemies with logic rather than loudness. His managers discovered they could bring out the fighter in Mundt by reporting bits of vicious criticism being used by the opposition. Responding to this kind of stimuli, Mundt would overpower his audiences with the logic and vehemence of his presentation.

The late Senator Henry Dvorshak of Idaho was a likeable, friendly man with a tremendous understanding of Idaho's needs. He was an effective Senator, but all his years in politics had not conditioned him to accept ingratitude as the normal payment for a service performed. Dvorshak, who was intensely loyal to the interests of Idaho, expected the people of Idaho to reciprocate that loyalty. It grieved him when they didn't and he made no attempt to conceal his grief.

Every public servant has a right now and then to complain about the lack of genuine public appreciation for services rendered. But this became almost an obsession with Dvorshak. As a result he found it difficult to make a decision. The thought that the people wouldn't understand or appreciate what he did became a stumbling block which might very well have ended in a defeat in 1960.

John Martin, Dvorshak's able campaign manager, recognized his boss' preoccupation with this single ugly fact of political life was limiting Dvorshak's effectiveness. Martin deliberately fed the Senator's ego with words of well-deserved praise from some of Idaho's substantial citizens. He protected his boss from hearing the critics, and he assumed responsibility for making all of the vexing decisions.

Martin sent the Senator to a state Republican convention in Twin Falls armed with the information that factions were threatening party unity and, if permitted to continue unchecked, would probably lead to a Democrat sweep in November. Dvorshak had a cause he loved—the Republican Party. His personal problems became insignificant, and this great old warrior waded into that convention. He laid it on the line to his fellow party members. In blunt, unmistakable language his words, like a surgeon's scalpel, excised the swollen egos that threatened to produce disaster.

Then he gave the convention a cause—and the cause wasn't Henry Dvorshak or his re-election to the Senate. The cause was the endurance of the Republic, the perpetuation of the political faith of the Republican Party. The image of Henry Dvorshak was preserved—a big, friendly, smiling man who had given all of his energy and all of his ability in the service of a principle he held more important than personalities.

Keeping in mind that the indifferent voter is the one who must be reached, it should be obvious that it will be difficult to claim the attention of this indifferent voter long enough to impress him with all of the virtues or assets of your candidate. It is necessary to make a selection. In making this choice contrast becomes all-important.

The indifferent citizen will respond favorably when the image of your candidate is easily recognizable as something totally different from the image of your candidate's opponent. The shades of gray have little significance. It is the black and the white which must be emphasized.

Political billboards are distressingly similar. The voter must choose between two men who wear the same kind of clothes, put their trousers on one leg at a time, talk about the same things, and are both appearing before the constituency asking for votes. Really, candidates are monotonously alike.

To assist the indifferent citizen in his task of recognizing your candidate is going to be a difficult assignment, but this is the primary task of the campaign manager. A good place to start is with the campaign photograph.

Most candidates want the photographer to make them look handsome, young, well groomed and friendly.

The photographer should be instructed to produce a photograph of your candidate which reflects the image you have developed. If the people think of your candidate as young and strong, friendly and informal, the official photographs can reflect this image. If your candidate is considered experienced, the cameraman who understands his assignment can capture wisdom and experience in the candidate's photograph. Don't be content with just one picture; have a different photograph for each facet of the candidate's image and use the proper picture at the proper time.

The photograph to be used on the outdoor billboard is extremely important. Voters whizzing by at 50 mph don't have time to read more than five or six words. But if the photograph projects the image you want displayed, the impression of the picture can do the job.

Republican Congressman John Rhodes of Arizona is of something less than average height. He wears his hair in a crewcut. He is a determined, industrious worker for the people of his district but no on would accuse him of being a matinee idol. One of the most effective campaign photographs I have seen was a full-length figure of John Rhodes carrying a briefcase. He wasn't standing still, he was moving. (A good cameraman can give action to a still photo.) The billboard said: "He knows your way around Washington."

The impact was tremendous. The picture said it all. Here was a vigorous, determined man on the job. His opponent in that campaign was a very handsome man. His billboards carried what I would call a "collar-ad photograph." The contrast was tremendous. Here was a black and white difference screaming to be recognized . . . John Rhodes, the worker, busy on the job. His handsome opponent, almost in repose, was just waiting to be admired.

As the profile of your candidate is developed and the profile of his opponent is developed, it will be easy to discover numerous areas of black and white contrast and the physical differences are quite as important as political differences.

If your candidate is younger than his opponent, you have the opposites of young and old. If your candidate is more experienced than his opponent, you have the black and white contrast of the beginner and the expert just waiting to be exploited. Farmer versus city man; professional politician versus concerned citizen; successful lawyer versus the perennial aspirant for public office; a native of the constituency versus a newcomer —the list of opposites which can be emphasized is almost inexhaustible.

The research efforts will keep you supplied with samples of your opponent's printing. Be sure that yours is different. In radio, television and newspaper strive to find a format which will identify the cause of your candidate before a word is spoken or a single line of type is added.

Never attempt to beat the other man at his own game. If the opponent possesses a great deal more experience in public life, don't argue that your candidate is experienced. To do so creates a situation comparable to that when a Sunday golfer challenges a touring pro.

In the California campaign which found Helen Gahagan Douglas and Richard Nixon contesting for a seat in the United States Senate, Mrs. Douglas was the champion of increased welfare benefits and federal benevolence. Nixon was the tough-minded, aggressive anti-communist. Nixon couldn't attempt to compete with Mrs. Douglas as a champion of public welfare. When Mrs. Douglas tried to contend that she was just as anti-communist as her opponent, it was the Sunday golfer challenging the touring pro.

Dick Nixon won that contest and went on to become Vice President of the United States, but his enemies have never forgiven him for choosing the single issue which put Mrs. Douglas at great disadvantage. Friends of the defeated candidate still maintain that Nixon smeared his opponent. What he did, according to his campaign manager, Murray Chotiner, was to concentrate on the issue. In case after case Dick Nixon told audiences: "I have been advised not to talk about communism, but I am going to tell the people of California the truth and this is one thing we cannot stop talking about as long as the menace of international communism faces us here in the United States."

Nixon led the way in the exposure of Alger Hiss. His knowledge and his competence in this field made the subject a natural one for him and the voters reacted precisely as manager Chotiner hoped they would.

When the voters see the wrong image of the candidate, the campaign is headed for disaster. In the Douglas-Nixon California campaign the voters, according to Chotiner, saw Mrs. Douglas as a member of Congress who had voted with Vito Marcantonio more often than any other member. Chotiner printed this record on paper with a pinkish tinge and he says: "We had more requests and demands for this literature than any other." The electorate saw Mrs. Douglas not as a brilliant, compassionate member of Congress, but rather as someone who had voted consistently with Vito Marcantonio, a prominent left-winger.

In the 1952 race for the Senate seat in Arizona, McFarland saw his opponent Goldwater as a well-to-do, department store owner and a dilettante in politics. We made the voters see Goldwater as a serious, determined, young man. McFarland, who was the Majority Leader under Truman, was presented to the voters as a henchman and supporter of Harry. We hammered away at Truman's Korean war, a conflict which was then dragging into a stalemate because the foreign policy makers in Washington refused to permit the military commanders in the field freedom of action.

Our "Burma-Shave" jingle signs read: "Mac is for Harry. Harry's all through. You be for Barry . . . 'Cause Barry's for you."

Goldwater won by 6,727 votes.

In the 1958 gubernatorial race in Arizona, our Republican candidate was a young, recently retired businessman who had never served in any political office. His opponent was the successful, incumbent attorney general. The Republican Fannin was presented to the voters as a successful, determined businessman eager to bring his knowledge of business administration to bear upon the fiscal affairs of Arizona. His opponent saw Fannin as a neophyte, an awkward, inexperienced politician and we actually capitalized on Fannin's lack of political history.

When all the planning has been completed, when the manager and the candidate and the campaign staff are in agreement on the image of the candidate, the next requirement is consistency.

In every campaign the voters try to determine a theme. The theme of the campaign and the image of the candidate govern the selection and creation of every piece of printed material, dictate the speeches to be written, and provide the criteria for making a judgment on that perennial question: "Is this action necessary?"

A candidate can never bring the necessary amount of objectivity to the contemplation of those efforts being conducted in his behalf. The candidate is not competent because of his deep personal involvement to make the necessary vital decisions on strategy. The campaign management must make these decisions. And the campaign management must keep the candidate in character.

Time after time the voters in a particular constituency have elected a man to public office in recognition of his virtues and his faults. Poor public speakers have often been victorious. Men with little outward polish have been chosen. Individuals with a narrow viewpoint centered on a concern for the lives and problems of their neighbors have been chosen. And then what happens? The earnest, dull, poor public speaker begins to conceive of himself as an orator. The humorless student of the constituency's problems tries to be witty. The plain man puts on polish and when he stands before the voters for re-election, his fellow citizens are bewildered—for this is not the man to whom they gave their confidence in the first place.

Keep your candidate in character. If he is an incumbent, don't toss away or minimize those attractive qualities which contributed to his first election.

Members of the Congress of the United States are probably

the best informed people in the world on a magnificent variety of issues and problems. Their official responsibilities give them access to a great deal of knowledge which is denied to the public. They sit on select committees and benefit from the best brains in the scientific world. They are briefed repeatedly on the intricacies of foreign relations. They are a living, functioning part of the organism of government. And all of these things can be dangerous.

The candidate who has just returned to his home state after hearing a briefing on some new superior weapons system is almost irresistibly tempted to share this special knowledge with the first audience he encounters. But if the audience is not interested in the subject, the candidate's knowledge can backfire.

When Abraham Lincoln was campaigning for the Presidency of the United States he played on a single theme—slavery. Lincoln, as a practicing Whig, had many strong convictions about the proper role of government. Certainly he must have been tempted to speak about the subjects which held great interest for him, but the people were concerned over the slavery question and Lincoln wisely addressed all of his remarks to what was the major concern of his constituents.

If in our journey into the realities of political campaigning you may have gained the impression that this political jungle is a world of make-believe where the tricks of the trade can produce victory, put aside that misconception. A campaign is deadly serious. What we have discovered here is nothing more than a collection of complexities. The image of the candidate must be a genuine image. If the candidate is not possessed of quality, no amount of manipulation can give him quality. If the candidate is not concerned with the great issues of his people, no amount of campaign paraphernalia can cause the electorate to take his candidacy seriously. Serious effort is required to develop an understanding of the image of the candidate. Serious effort will also be required to identify the overriding issues. This assignment will be discussed in the chapter on polls and surveys.

There is a logical sequence which must be followed in the development of a successful campaign and image is either at the top or nearly at the top of the list. Once the campaign group has determined the image of the candidate, every campaign activity and every individual connected with the campaign must concentrate on the presentation and enhancement of that image.

5 | Aspirations and Expectations

What is the irresistible lure which brings men by the millions to sporting events? Is it merely to see an exhibition of physical power? Or to witness bodily contact between two great athletes? Indeed, this may be a part of it, but only a small part. Partisan man comes to the sporting event in the expectation and the hope of seeing his team or his champion victorious.

Men cling tenaciously to each rung on the economic ladder. Only a few dull clods are content with merely holding onto their perch. Most of us are reaching for a higher rung. The devout Christian endures the cruel world of today resting upon God's promise of something better when this life is finished. But even the devout Christian hopes for an improvement in the world tomorrow.

Political campaigns which offer no hope of improvement attract few supporters. The candidate who does not indicate by his words and his actions that his election will bring measurable improvement to the lot of the body politic has small chance of success.

We speak with a certain cynicism of campaign promises and this phrase has become synonymous with insincere commitments in every walk of life.

The candidate who out-promises or over-promises runs the risk of having his deceit penetrated by the voters, but every campaign platform, indeed, every political statement, contains the implicit suggestion that if the author of the statement is given the authority of public office, certain desirable actions will take place.

The candidate who proclaims loudly that he has made no promises is, in fact, making a greater promise for he is declaring that he will be independent if elected, unhindered by prior pledges bartered for the support of some segment of the voting population.

A clear understanding of the part promises play in any political campaign can produce a state of magnificent frustration. Yet, in our recent memory Eisenhower was elected on his two great promises: "to clean up the mess in Washington," "to go to Korea."

Kennedy was elected on his promise "to get the country moving again." The element which must be understood is the requirement to limit the campaign promises of your candidate to the discernible major aspirations of the voting public.

In contests for the United States Senate or for the House of Representatives, promises are frequently explicit. Candidate Jones will get such-and-such a dam for his district. Candidate Smith will bring defense plants to the state. Candidate Brown will be an economizer. Candidate Green will fight communism. The trouble begins when Candidate Black promises to economize in one breath, to bring more federal spending into the state with another; to reduce the expenditures for military hardware while at the same time he plans to support an expansion of the defense capabilities.

The problem of what to promise and what not to promise haunts every campaign manager. Candidates frequently succumb to the irresistible temptation of saying what they think the audience wants to hear, and unless the whole area of promise has been carefully defined in advance, even the most experienced politicians will now and then find themselves in boiling hot water.

The changing whims and passions of the people make it virtually impossible for any politician to respond affirmatively to every seemingly popular demand. The great strength of the American constitutional system has been its built-in resistance to the fickle moods of the sovereign voter. All of the republics of France have suffered great injury because theirs was a plebiscitery system. The English parliamentary procedure bestows upon the ruling administration certain advantage in that it is possible for the minister in power to call for elections at moments most propitious to his cause. The calendar rule of the American Republic makes a certain consistency of position compatible with the problems of election.

To be effective your candidate must be consistent. Since on minor matters and specific issues men of good conscience frequently find it necessary to alter a prior opinion, it is important not to permit these questions of passing importance any room on the schedule of promises your candidate offers.

Every citizen who will vote in the next election, dated from the time you read these words, hopes to see the tax burden imposed by the government lessened. The more realistic recognize that taxes have always increased and never substantially decreased, but even these cannot stifle an aspiration for that day when the necessary costs of government will be lessened and the amount of the tax collected reduced.

We can't have it both ways. We can't have increased federal activity and expenditure and reduced taxes at the same time. In every constituency there is a real or imagined need for some new federal operation, be it nothing more than a new and larger post office. What then should be the attitude of your candidate toward this fundamental problem? Before finding an answer it will be necessary for the campaign manager and the candidate to become extremely familiar with the budgetary requirements in the area of government the candidate aspires to serve. The most adamant pinch-penny among the voters you hope to reach will respond favorably if your candidate can discuss intelligently and with authority the reasons behind the current tax rate.

A study of any governmental budget—school district, county, state or federal—will reveal several areas open to question. When these are identified and understood, your candidate can with great consistency discuss these items and recommend sensible reductions in expenditures. If your candidate is basically oriented toward the philosophy which argues in favor of increased governmental spending, his attempt to wear the mantle of an economizer by picking upon some particularly flagrant wasteful activity will be recognized by the voter as mere pretense. Therefore, before the manager and the candidate can determine what the campaign promise should be in regard to spending, it is necessary for the candidate to adopt without equivocation one or the other of the alternative viewpoints.

If your candidate's conscience requires that he support an increase in governmental activities, then his promises can be specific and persuasive when he outlines the benefits that will accrue to the voter if the spending programs are implemented. In the event your candidate makes this decision, you can actually gain favor with the voters by admitting that the promised benefits are going to cost them additional money.

Nelson Rockefeller, when elected governor of New York State, was immediately pressured to increase certain programs of the state government. Governor Rockefeller found the programs desirable and supported them, but he also made it clear that taxes would be increased to pay for the programs. The spender who resorts to borrowing or who pretends that additional benefits can be obtained without additional government costs is soon branded a hypocrite.

In another chapter we will describe a method for determining the major concerns or primary interests of a constituency. The promises made by your candidate should deal in honest and determined fashion with your candidate's approach to the major concerns of those voters whose support he is seeking.

Since the development of the federal welfare program we have created a numerically large group of individuals who are dependent upon the federal program for all or part of their income. These people can be expected to give their vote to the candidate who offers them the best deal in terms of their welfare support.

Some elections have been won with the solid support of groups segregated by economic or geographical situations, but in most campaigns these special interest voters are not strong enough to determine the outcome. The problem is, and always will be, to resist every temptation to try to promise every voter what you think that voter wants.

It does not require the service of a crystal ball to determine the aspirations of the American people. The national character reveals that Americans want to be free, hope to be prosperous, long for a world at peace, and want to believe that the men they select for public office possess ability, character and integrity.

All of your campaign promises really serve the same end: to convince the voter that your candidate has the ability to understand the problems, has a character strong enough to work for a happy solution, and possesses sufficient integrity to be safely entrusted with the power of public office.

There are two kinds of promises, a promise to do something, to perform a service or to support a particular philosophical position; or a promise *not* to do something, to oppose a particular concept or philosophical position. The negative promise is an easier one to make and to keep and because some people are more influenced to vote *against* than to vote *in favor of* the negative promise deserves particular study and attention.

Incumbent office holders usually find it more convenient to complement the record of their past performance with a promise of future action. Candidates challenging an incumbent usually find it necessary to criticize the record of the incumbent. This

criticism becomes more meaningful when the candidate couples
it with a pledge that if he is successful he will not do what his
incumbent opponent has done.

Frequently the most effective of the "I will not" promises
have to do with relatively trivial errors committed by the opposition. From the voting record of your opponent, your candidate is able to show that the man he is trying to replace missed
a certain number of votes. His promise is coupled with this
disclosure—he maintains that if he is elected to office, he will
take care of the store and be there when it is time to vote.

In one Mid-Western state where an incumbent governor was
seeking re-election, about the only real criticism his opponent
could make was that the incumbent had used the services of a
highway patrolman to drive the governor's official car to and
from meetings around the state. At most, there was nothing
more involved than the highway patrolman's salary, a matter
of $500 or $600 a month. The total budget for that state was
well over $250 million dollars a year, but the challenging can-
didate made a great point of the chauffeur-driven car and
promised that, if elected, he would not force the taxpayers to
hire a chauffeur for him.

All this was a clear appeal to greed and envy, but it was
couched in terms readily understandable and the voter who was
having a hard time paying his taxes and living on a small income
resented the governor's acceptance of this small luxury. The
incumbent was defeated.

In 1911 Henry Fountain Ashurst was elected to the United
States Senate from Arizona. Ashurst was a florid politician
of the old school who affected a swallow-tailed coat and a string
tie. He was a magnificent orator, a good politician; he took
scrupulous care of his constituents and they took good care of
him at election time.

In 1940, with the clouds of war so visible, Henry Ashurst
remained in Washington as Chairman of the Senate Judiciary
Committee. He had an obligation to the nation which in his

mind was more important than a six-month campaign for re-election in Arizona. Ashurst was confident the people whom he had served so well would approve his decision.

An unknown politician, a judge from one of the state's small population counties, decided to run against Ashurst in the Democrat Party primary. The incumbent Senator was not vulnerable to attack for anything he had done or failed to do in Washington. His opponent shrewdly exploited the only possible avenue for victory. He traveled the state, appearing as speaker at non-political meetings and visiting with his fellow Democrats. Invariably he asked: "How long has it been since you've seen Henry Ashurst?" That's all. No criticisms. No comment. Just the question which implied that Henry Ashurst was no longer interested in visiting the citizens of his state.

The promise was there—the promise that if the people wanted a senator who cared about them, who was interested enough in their thinking and their welfare to visit with them, then it was time for a change. And change they did. Ashurst was defeated and Ernest McFarland was elected.

Be leery of the specific promise. Your candidate can, without fear, commit himself to a philosophical promise. He can say that the federal government should demand an hour's work for every hour of wages paid. But if you let him suggest that federal wages are too high and should be reduced, all those on the federal payroll will oppose him; and should he be elected, the chances are that at some point in the future your candidate will have to reverse himself on that position. The spiraling economy argues against such specific commitments.

Goldwater, elected in '52 as a candidate who opposed increased federal expenditures, drew strong critical fire when, shortly after his election, he voted for a raise in postal rates.

The platform is a general collection of promises, specific and implied. When your candidate's platform is being prepared, ask him if he means to keep the promises—if it is within his power to keep the promises.

Since the wide-spread development of membership in the John Birch Society, we have had numerous candidates whose political beliefs embrace all the actions of the Blue Book. "We must take the United States out of the United Nations." Ah! This statement is a promise, a promise that, if elected, the Birch candidate can be expected to work toward the withdrawal of the United States from that world-peace organization.

It is obvious that one senator could not take the United States out of the United Nations. One senator demanding our withdrawal from the U.N. would find very little support in the Senate as that body is constituted in 1964. This kind of promise reveals the maker as either an immature, impractical dreamer or a faker of the first order. John Birch-thinking candidates could take much of the curse off their extremist position if they would confine themselves to sponsoring objectives within the realm of practical achievement.

Senators have been elected on "share-the-wealth" platforms and "every-man-a-king" platitudes, but they are not often re-elected on such obviously absurd promises.

Someone will object that no politician is in a position to guarantee delivery unless he be elected President of the United States—and even in that office there are limitations on personal power. Yet there are, indeed, many promises which will satisfy the aspirations and expectations of the electorate and are well within the area of delivery. A candidate who espouses a particular legislative solution to a particular problem can promise to introduce a measure in the Congress aimed at accomplishing that objective.

At one time the question of whether or not to repeal the Connally reservation had political significance in a number of areas. Candidates on either side of the question were provided with an opportunity to make a promise which they could keep: "I will vote against the removal of the Connally reservation," or "I will vote for the removal of the Connally reservation."

In many Western states, the so-called right-to-work laws

which are state rather than federal legislation have enlisted violent support and violent criticism. Partisans were eager to have all candidates for public office commit themselves on the right-to-work issue. In such an area, no promise should be expected or made by a candidate for the Congress or a candidate for governor since the matter is specifically within the province of the state legislators.

Every candidate can make certain promises of a personal nature that will make him more acceptable to the voters. Promises having to do with the candidate's intentions toward the voters after election are extremely important and commitments to love them as deeply in December as he did in October have paved the way to office for numerous public figures.

Promises have to do with honor, and honor is a moral state. A candidate who promises to benefit one segment of the constituency at the expense of another is making an immoral promise and, even if the obligation is never kept, such a course of action leads to disillusionment for the voters.

In many areas it is impossible to out-promise the opposition. The old saw: "I'll do everything he'll do for you, only I'll do it better" has not produced many victories on election day. Promises that only announce a moral commitment that every American implicitly or explicitly makes by virtue of being an American citizen are dangerous. A politician who says: "I'll tell you the truth" may be trying to imply that his opponent is a liar. But we expect our public figures to speak the truth and such a promise cannot be exchanged for votes at the ballot box.

Be sure your candidate can keep the promises he makes.

Be sure the promises relate to the major concerns of the constituency.

Be sure the promises are consistent with the character and image of your candidate.

Be sure the promises deal realistically with the anticipations and the expectations of the voters.

6 | Timing

Political contests capture the public interest because they offer the citizen an opportunity to be both spectator and participant. The rival candidates are the acknowledged competitors. But as the campaign progresses and the tempo increases, partisan supporters become in a large measure personal combatants. These citizen supporters carry the fight to the enemy. They defend the candidate who enjoys their affections and on election day their vote helps to decide the issue.

The season of politics extends by tradition from Labor Day to the first Tuesday after the first Monday in November. In any contest where there is a primary to determine the candidate, the season may be extended by anywhere from four to six months. Successful campaigns are usually set in motion at least a year in advance of the decision date, and many candidates establish their organizations eighteen to twenty months in advance of that day.

Because the struggle for victory at the polls lacks that splendid unity which distinguishes a championship prize fight or a championship football game, the timing of the effort is all important.

For the candidate and his manager each contest—no matter how humble the office sought—is a championship affair. The

63

candidate isn't required to win so many preliminary bouts to go after the grand prize. He is not judged on his season's average. The shadow of defeat will last for at least two years and in some areas it may be four or six years before the defeated candidate has a chance to go after the prize he lost.

In many aspects of the conduct of a political campaign the manager is required to do the best with the tools he is given. Only so much money is available—never quite enough to do all the things a manager would like to do. Candidates can't be selected the way beauty queens are chosen—for their appearance, grace, personality, talent, etc. The manager must take whatever qualities the candidate possesses and exploit them.

The area of conflict where the victory must be won is frequently dictated by forces over which the manager has no control. In some elections an ethnic group holds the key to victory, or sectional interest may make the final decision. Bad weather can keep enough voters at home to make the difference. But in the matter of timing the manager is a free agent.

Timing alone cannot win every campaign. Too many other factors influence the final outcome. But in my experience poor timing must be named as the major cause of most political defeats.

Public enthusiasm is a fragile, ephemeral thing. No amount of public opinion sampling can prove conclusively "what might have been." Many qualified political analysts believe that if the 1948 presidential election had been held in early October instead of November, Tom Dewey would have been the victor instead of Harry Truman. In that effort the Dewey managers allowed their candidate to peak too early.

Dewey began the campaign well in the lead. Truman, who had inherited the Presidency upon the death of Franklin D. Roosevelt, was regarded as a political accident and there was every indication to believe the people wanted a change. Truman in his forthright and sometimes profane way began to attack the record of the 80th Congress. Dewey refused to defend the Congress, apparently believing that he might offend some section of the electorate. The polls put Dewey way in front. One commentator has said that Dewey campaigned as though he were already President. Truman, the acknowledged underdog, probably benefited from a sympathy vote. At any rate, he confounded all the pollsters and won re-election.

The key to timing a major political contest successfully is acceleration. It doesn't really matter where the candidate stands in the public affection at the start of a campaign. What does matter is that the candidate gain some new supporters every day.

To understand the importance of timing we must keep in mind constantly that if the candidate is to win, he must reach and persuade no more than twenty or twenty-five per cent of the electorate. These are the Indifferents who will oftentimes select one candidate over another just because they want to be with the winner.

The indifferent voter lives on the periphery of our real world. He may be, and very frequently is, a solid citizen—law abiding, productive, but apathetic in his attitude toward political decision. Many of the voters in this class have professions or jobs which absorb all of their interest. Until the past few years most doctors felt they were too busy to be interested in politics. Professional golfers who follow the tournament tours must devote all of their energy and attention to playing golf and very few of them have any time at all to give to any other interest. Men whose jobs keep them constantly traveling find it difficult to identify with local issues and local candidates. This group of indifferent voters will remain untouched and uninfluenced by the clamor of a political campaign until moments before it is necessary to make a decision.

Political campaigns generate their most strident sounds as the climactic day of decision approaches. No matter when the campaign is formally opened, the manager must plan his maximum efforts for the final two weeks.

In the 1952 Arizona Goldwater-McFarland contest the poll

takers never once indicated that Goldwater was in the lead. The final sampling was taken two and a half weeks before election day. Goldwater won that election in those two and a half weeks.

In 1960 in South Dakota, Karl Mundt defeated his Democrat opponent, George McGovern, in the final days of that contest.

This necessity for acceleration has a great bearing on the allocation of campaign funds. As a general rule one-half of the campaign funds available should be allocated for expenditure during the first three-quarters of the time available, with the second half of the campaign money being spent in the last one-quarter of the available time. Frequently, commitments must be made in advance and this will be discussed in detail in the chapter on Mass Media.

The candidate's schedule of personal appearances should be arranged so that he will be seen by the largest audiences in the final weeks. This can readily be accomplished by sending your candidate to the less populous areas of the constituency during the early days of the campaign, bringing him into the big urban centers in the final weeks. (A device for increasing the effectiveness of these final appearances will be discussed in the chapter devoted to the proper use of television and radio.)

If elections were always decided on rational issues or upon the competence of the candidates or as an expression of an allegiance to a profound political philosophy, timing would undoubtedly be less important.

Frequently the methods employed by an astute campaign manager to accelerate the campaign are not apparent to the voters. In one campaign my strategy for increasing the pace was misunderstood by some and bitterly condemned by others.

Most candidates distribute bumper strips or windshield stickers to their followers. A moving automobile provides an excellent place for the display of the candidate's name. It can be assumed that if a citizen plasters his car with the candidate's name, he intends to vote for that candidate. The distribution of these stickers will give the activists in the citizen groups supporting your candidate a chance to satisfy their desire for physical participation.

I have been experimenting with various types of car stickers since 1938. Bumper strips are more popular now than they were when I first commenced my political activities. The quality of printing is better and the adhesive has been improved. Bumper strips available today will defy the elements and frustrate anyone who deliberately attempts to remove them. But bumper strips are expensive.

A colorful gummed sticker with the printing on the gummed side of the paper can be installed on the inside of an automobile rear window. (In many states it is illegal to put them on the windshield.) Protected by the glass, the sticker becomes an eye-level miniature billboard. The ones I have used have been about two inches high by eight inches long.

Traditional politicians will object to this size on the ground that it is not big enough to carry the candidate's full name. This is true. But the manager's job is to make his candidate a first-name friend of every voter. I believe the use of first names on the window stickers gives the candidate a real advantage. The first time I used this was for a candidate running for sheriff whose first name was Cal. The sticker said: "I'm for Cal."

In 1958 I decided to use a white gummed sticker printed with blue letters carrying the legend: "I'm for Barry." The *for* was very small type and *Barry* covered about two-thirds of the surface. We had estimated that at least 325,000 voters would go to the polls in that election so I ordered 250,000 of the blue and white stickers printed, to be delivered to me the first day of September. The printer kept his promise but I didn't distribute the stickers until the first week in October. My refusal to depart from the timing schedule brought the wrath of the gods down on my head.

Goldwater had announced his candidacy for re-election in the early spring. He was unopposed in the primary and so we decided to start the major public effort the week following Labor Day. In July and August Goldwater covered the outlying communities in the state, went to coffees in small towns, appeared before luncheon clubs in out-of-the-way communities. But our billboards, our major television, our radio and our newspaper efforts were all scheduled for September, October and the first week in November.

Early in the summer the Goldwater supporters began asking for bumper strips. At first I was able to put aside these requests merely by saying we would have them later. But when we officially opened the campaign the clamor for bumper strips or stickers increased.

Mrs. Emery Johnson, a very talented and wonderful woman who was serving as an elected member of the Republican National Committee from Arizona, made a trip from Tucson to my office in Phoenix to demand a supply of bumper stickers.

I explained to Mrs. Johnson that bumper strips and car window stickers attract a maximum of attention when they first appear. After a few days or a few weeks they become just another part of the automobile—like the radio aerial or the bumper guard or the license plate.

"Did you read every license plate on the cars you passed or met coming up here?" I asked.

"Of course not," she said.

"Did you see any cars without a license plate?"

After a moment's reflection, she said, "Yes, just as I was coming into Chandler, but it was a new car."

She had proved my point. She had seen all the license plates on all the cars because she was accustomed to seeing license plates. She had seen them without really giving them any attention. The unusual situation of a car without a plate had attracted her interest.

"We're going to distribute window stickers," I told her, "the first week in October. They will be on the cars for less than five weeks and nobody will have enough time to become accustomed to them.

"I'm going to try to have these on all the cars within the time span of five days. We believe this will heighten the impact tremendously."

My plan for distribution was rather simple. I mailed two stickers, together with a letter from Barry Goldwater, to every registered Republican in the state. The letter thanked them for everything they had done and then asked one additional favor: "Would you please put one of these stickers on your car and ask a friend to use the second sticker? It will be most helpful if you will do it before October 4."

Bumper strips cost about $40 a thousand. The gummed stickers cost us less than $5 per thousand. We would not have been able to finance such a widespread distribution of bumper strips. They are too big to be mailed in an ordinary envelope. Our total cost for the window stickers, the letter, the envelope and the postage was about $35 a thousand.

The results were extremely satisfactory. Five days after the stickers were mailed, anyone observing the flow of traffic, anywhere in the state of Arizona, must have believed that Goldwater supporters were in the majority. The effect of the appearance of the car stickers on our opponent and his supporters exceeded my most optimistic anticipation. Gloom and despair spread through his campaign office. One individual in the opposition camp must have been driving in a real nest of "I'm for Barry" cars. He came to work one morning to report that six out of every ten automobile owners in Arizona intended to vote for Goldwater. As far as he was concerned, the election was lost.

Ten days after we distributed the stickers I had a count made of the cars in parking lots and shopping centers in the greater Phoenix area. In some of the locations the "I'm for Barry" greatly outnumbered the McFarland cars. But when the reports for the day were totaled, we found that twenty-eight per cent of the cars had McFarland stickers, twenty-nine per cent of the cars had Goldwater stickers and forty-three per cent of the cars didn't have any stickers at all.

The McFarland stickers had been out for a least eight weeks

at the time the count was made. It was the timing of our distribution which gave impact to our use of the stickers. The appearance of the Goldwater signs within one week created an impression of strength out of all proportion to the actual number of stickers used.

The campaign manager should gear his efforts to reach maximum effectiveness in the forty-eight hour period before election day. This is a narrow and difficult target. It is much better to be twenty-four or forty-eight hours early than to be even twelve hours too late. But a campaign which reaches its peak a week to ten days ahead of election can bring disaster. Public affection is never static. *A candidate is always gaining or losing.* A campaign manager can learn a great deal about the fickle public by attending any top-notch sporting event.

World Series fans are usually extremely partisan. Thousands of people who come to the baseball park to cheer "their Dodgers" will actually boo and jeer if the performance of the Dodgers is lackluster or marked with error. The "fans" in a political contest, like the fans in the stadium, want to win. They want to see action.

A political candidate must hit home runs in the eighth and ninth innings if he is to retain the enthusiastic support of the indifferent voters until the moment the winner is determined. Since there are no umpires, no scoreboard, nothing but a final total to determine the winner, it becomes the responsibility of the campaign manager to plan the home runs.

Proper scheduling of the advertising media and the candidate appearances will give the mechanical acceleration required. Developing the "home-run hit" is a task for the manager.

In the 1962 congressional elections President Kennedy and his advisers skillfully exploited the presence of Russian missiles in Cuba. Kennedy hit a veritable barrage of over-the-fence home runs when he established the naval blockade and ordered Khrushchev to remove the weapons.

The Cuban type of made-to-order international situation

which can be cleverly exploited is not always present toward the end of a political campaign.

In 1952 Dwight Eisenhower was battling for the finish line when his managers provided him with a real home-run statement. The war in Korea had been dragging, casualties were increasing, the American public was clearly expressing its impatience with this no-decision war.

Candidate Eisenhower did not condemn our entry into the Korean conflict. He didn't challenge President Truman's judgment. To be openly critical of an American military effort would have been extremely offensive to the parents and relatives of the men who were dying in battle. His managers skillfully avoided all of the possible liability. Their candidate simply said: "If I am elected, I will go to Korea."

This magnificent home-run statement, coming from a highly respected military leader, captured the imagination and the loyalty of thousands of voters. It implied action, it aroused the nation's hopes and it was unanswerable by the opposition.

On that final day in November we all put our "X" in the square beside a man's name. Outwardly our act is an evidence of choice or decision between two human beings. Frequently a clever campaign effort avoids a head-on clash between the two candidates and instead permits the winner to run against an idea or a concept or a situation. In 1932 the Democrats made President Herbert Hoover personally responsible for the great depression. Roosevelt ran as much against the economic distress which then existed as he did against Hoover. In '36 and again in '40 Roosevelt's campaign strategists recalled the horror of the depression and made it synonomous with the Republican Party.

In the Goldwater-Arizona campaign of 1952 we identified our opponent as a close confident and associate of President Harry Truman. We campaigned against the "Truman scandals," the "Truman profanity" and "Truman's Korean War."

In the Goldwater 1958 campaign we emphasized the irrefutable fact that out-of-state labor leaders wanted to see Goldwater defeated, coupled our opponent with these out-of-state labor leaders and then aimed our big guns at the past and present misdeeds of monopoly labor unions.

Our research division paid close attention to the activities of all union officials in Arizona. We were particularly interested in finding and identifying anyone who might be properly described as an emissary of out-of-state labor interests.

Arizona is not a labor state. Most of the union members in Goldwater's constituency work at the construction trades. These are the craft unions—carpenters, bricklayers, electrical workers, stationary engineers and teamsters.

Arizona's great industrial development has been in the area of electronics and aircraft components—products that utilize a highly skilled, technically trained labor force. (The vertical unionism of the Auto Workers type has never really caught on in Arizona.) A very high percentage of these people are college graduates whose training in technical skills would find them employment anywhere. We believed if Goldwater could be presented as a candidate who was championing the freedom of the individual worker and challenging the dictatorial orders of the union bosses, we could arouse sympathetic support.

In May of 1958 our research people advised us that a West Coast labor leader had established headquarters in a Tucson hotel. This man, the regional representative for the Political Action group of the AFL-CIO, immediately contacted labor officials in Arizona who introduced him to a number of labor-endorsed political candidates.

When the AFL-CIO COPE organization met in Miami, Florida, in the spring of 1958, the newspapers reported that organized labor would make Goldwater its number one target. COPE would provide the brains, the muscle and the money to defeat this Senator whose constant questions were a continual embarrassment to the leaders of the labor movement.

Most Americans resent being told what to do. Orders coming from out of state are deeply resented. If the voters in any constituency somehow come to believe that an out-of-state expert or a representative of out-of-state interests is intruding in their political quarrels by telling them how to vote, an angry, negative response is predictable.

The resentment we provoked in response to the labor leaders' declaration against Goldwater was not based on any general antipathy toward the leaders personally. We would have been just as successful had their statement come from the President of the United States Steel Company or from the Chairman of Americans for Democratic Action.

Because organized labor traditionally supports candidates of the Democrat Party, Republicans throughout the country have tried to make this union support a bogey man. The CIO, which is very resourceful in political matters, has developed an extremely effective technique for getting out the friendly vote. They even made a documentary training film called "The Wisconsin Story" to be used in instructing members enlisted for political action.

With the over-all strategy of our campaign in mind, the appearance of the regional union political officer in Arizona provided an opportunity to demonstrate the truth of our claim that out-of-state union bosses were organizing their resources to defeat Goldwater. But May of 1958 was not the time to do this. Had we exposed the presence of the out-of-state union official when we first discovered him, the exposure would have been ignored by many of the Indifferents who were not interested in politics in May. The effect would have been forgotten by November.

To make the most of this situation we had to time the disclosure—to key it in with the last few weeks of the campaign when the public's interest would peak. We kept our mouths shut and the research division began to expand its file on the activities of this non-resident union official.

By mid-summer we had developed quite a portrait of our visitor. He was a veteran of union organizational warfare with a record for violence which included at least one arrest by California police. Someone provided us with an official arrest photograph showing the identification numbers pinned on the suspect's chest.

During the summer months our visitor increased his activities —apparently in the belief that his presence in Arizona had gone completely unnoticed. He moved back and forth between Phoenix and Tucson and visited the labor temples in both cities with great regularity. A parade of political lesser-fry made their pilgrimages to this man's hotel room. Our research division heard that the purpose of these calls was to get union support. We had a real home run shocker—if we could prevent premature disclosure.

About the middle of October a member of our research team informed me that an alert newspaperman had been asking questions in the hotel where the union leader made his headquarters.

From my standpoint it was still too early to break the story. A campaign manager must deal constantly with reporters. It is his job to know the ones who can be trusted to keep a story confidential . . . he must also know the reporters who would sell their mother for a news beat.

The newsman who had been asking questions was extremely competent. I knew he would keep digging. The danger from our standpoint was that his inquiry would produce only such information as could be found in Arizona. If the union leader became aware of the newspaper's interest in his activities he might disappear. To give our planned exposé its maximum impact it was very important to keep the out-of-state union man with us until the day the story was scheduled to break.

I had no choice. I approached the reporter who had been asking questions. I told him he was on the trail of a really hot story and offered to make a bargain. "If you will wait one week, we will be able to give you the full story—the man's pedigree, his police photograph and a documented history of all of his

activities as a political agent in California and in Arizona. I
will give you a list of the local candidates who have been to
see him. I'll give you the dates and the times when he has consulted with labor officials in Arizona. And, if you want it, you
can have it on an exclusive basis."

The reporter's response was: "You sonofabitch. You've had
this story all along and been sitting on it."

"Not exactly sitting on it," I told him, "we've been developing it. Each day has produced some new information. And I
thought it would be better to give you the full story than to
break it too early and let our friend leave town before we had
the real dope."

The reporter said he would have to consult with his editor
and added, "You'd better come along with me."

In the editor's office I spelled out the whole story. I didn't
have the photographs or the list of contacts or the day-by-day
account of the visitor's travels in Arizona with me, but I could
recite most of these from memory. The story was so big the
editor didn't want it exclusively. I think he was afraid his
paper might be all alone. He knew the unions and the Democrat
Party officials who had been connected with this effort would
be extremely angry. He wanted every paper in the state to have
the story on an equal basis.

"If you have the facts to back up what you've told me," he
said, "this thing alone could swing the election. It'll push in the
Republican gubernatorial candidate right along with your Senator. And it might carry two or three other Republicans with
him."

We all recognized the possibility that some other enterprising
reporter might stumble on a lead to the story. It was agreed that
I would call a press conference in Phoenix at the end of the
following week. I would make all of the information available
to all of the state's daily newspapers and I would have pictures
and fact sheets and supporting detail for distribution at that time.

The story broke on Saturday—two weeks before election Tuesday, and only three days in advance of the ideal release date I had first established when the possibility of such exposure had first come to my attention.

An enterprising candid camera enthusiast had provided us with photographs of the union organizer in the company of Democrat Party state officials. These became front page art on every important newspaper in Arizona.

There was absolutely nothing illegal or immoral in the labor union's political activity. They had every right to send an expert in to assist the local officials. National political parties commonly engage in this kind of activity. Special interest groups other than the labor unions have their traveling experts constantly engaged in attempting to influence the outcome of an election. But in this case the union boss had moved with great secrecy. Democrat officials in Arizona had constantly denied they were receiving any help from organized labor and a number of opposition spokesmen had emphatically denied the charge that out-of-state political experts had been sent into Arizona by the unions to assist the Democrat candidates.

The story was a real shocker. The police record for an act of violence, the police photograph, the long history of political activity on behalf of labor unions, suddenly and dramatically illustrated one of our principal campaign themes.

We had said that out-of-state labor bosses would project themselves into the Arizona political contest to defeat Goldwater. The newspapers printed the truth of that prediction and the union aspect became almost incidental—the obvious resentment was against an "outsider" trying to tell the people of Arizona how to vote.

This experience made a lasting impression on me. When I became a consultant to the United States Senators running for re-election in 1960, my first resolve was to remain anonymous. I had remarked that other employees of the Republican Senatorial Campaign Committee often received publicity. It is absolutely legitimate for the campaign committees of the House and the Senate to send their agents anywhere in the nation to assist a national candidate. Both parties do this with great regularity. But no amount of legitimate authority can make an out-of-state expert an acceptable participant in a local election.

7 | Researching the Opposition

"Know thine enemy" is good advice any time. In a political contest it becomes an imperative. Professional football teams spend almost as much money and energy scouting the opponents as they do on developing their own game. And while we frequently think of our candidate as a member of the party's political team, the voters who will make the decision look upon the contest as a head-to-head battle.

No campaign manager, no candidate, can wage an intelligent offensive until he has equipped himself with every shred of available information about his opponent. The facts, collected and carefully catalogued, fall easily into four categories: 1. Personal information about the candidate and his associates; 2. The candidate's voting record or other public actions; 3. The voting habits or statistical summary of the constituency, precinct by precinct; 4. The issues.

In every political contest there is a semblance of effort to scout the opposition. In my experience most research is underfinanced, poorly organized, and totally lacking in the depth of detail necessary to make the effort worthwhile.

The research organization should be set up under the direct command of the campaign manager. Since a variety of information is desired, it is necessary to employ a research staff with highly specialized competence.

A librarian with the ability to organize the information so that it will be instantly available should be placed in charge of the files. A lawyer, newspaperman or someone skilled in investigating, who is capable of going behind the public information, should be selected to develop the personal history of the opposing candidate. A student of public affairs or a political scientist is best equipped to develop the voting records and the position papers. As issues arise during the campaign, the manager and the candidate will need intellectual support for their position and similarly they must know what authority supports the position taken by the opposition.

The investigator who is to build the file on the opposing candidate should also be assigned to a similar task in regard to everyone who is prominently associated with the opposition candidate.

A campaign manager who has available a complete dossier on all of the people in the opposition will frequently be able to predict accurately the kind of campaign that will be waged against his candidate.

"Know thine enemy" suggests that it is necessary to understand the psychological, economic and emotional forces that will be arrayed against your candidate.

The research task begins with newspaper and magazine clippings. It doesn't end there. If the man you are trying to beat is an incumbent holding high office, it may take several weeks to gather the available newspaper and magazine items.

Most newspapers keep a morgue—a reference file on individuals who have made news in the past. It is often difficult for an outsider to gain access to this information, particularly if the newspaper happens to be supporting your opponent. But it is always possible to find a friendly staffer who will provide photo copies of all the clips on file in his paper's morgue.

If no other source is available, search the public libraries. Bound copies of the state's newspapers will provide a day-to-day history of your opponent's activities. Some libraries will permit you to make a photo copy from the files. If this cannot be done, equip your researcher with dictating equipment and have the material transcribed.

Unknowns don't very often aspire to public office. It is always possible to find a record of your opponent's past in the daily press. This gathering of newspaper clippings is commonplace. Unfortunately, too many managers stop digging when they have exhausted the public sources of information.

How has your opponent made his living in the past? How much of the world's goods has he acquired? What are his family connections? What was his record in school? Business associates can provide valuable information if your opponent is in business. If he is a lawyer, your investigator should search out past clients, review the prominent cases in which your opponent has participated, gather the opinions of your opponent's contemporaries.

In one campaign we developed enough information to fill three standard size filing cabinets. This collection of newspaper clippings, photographs and confidential memos on our opponent and his close associates was indexed and cross-indexed. When the campaign was over and we were ready to dispose of the material, I had it weighed—123 pounds. I estimated that we had used in a specific way only seven items. But because of that mass of information, we were never taken off guard, and in two areas I could forecast accurately before the event the strategy our opponent would employ against us.

In one campaign research developed the information that a Mr. X, one of our opponent's most active supporters, had a political history in the Midwest. As the campaign developed, Mr. X became a particular thorn in our flesh—that is, he was an effective operator on behalf of our opponent. We sent an investigator to the man's former home and learned that he had at one time been publicly identified with a socialist newspaper. This information was passed along to a friendly reporter. As a result of the stories which appeared, Mr. X resigned his position as an official member of the opposition campaign staff and left town.

The possibility of a candidate being punished because of the sins of his associates is an ever-present angle. Our opponent didn't know about Mr. X and his socialist background. He should have checked Mr. X before accepting him as a volunteer member of his staff.

Most campaign groups are recruited from the close associates of the candidate. Long acquaintance makes it unnecessary to examine the qualifications or the loyalties of these people. In a state-wide campaign where a large organization is needed the wise manager will have his research people dig into the background of any unknown who offers to help the campaign in an official capacity.

The campaign manager must be extremely careful not to offend the voting public by allowing his candidate to appear to be aligned with any of the varied, semi-political organizations which have been formed in the past few years. If a member of Americans for Democratic Action becomes identified with your candidate, those in the body politic who disapprove of the ADA will transfer their disapproval to your candidate. Since 1960 the John Birch Society has stimulated a great many people to political action. The inclusion of a John Birch member in an official campaign organization would adversely affect those who disapprove of the society. A known communist, a professional labor agitator, an individual who has been prominently identified with some highly emotional public question such as segregation or integration, right to work, anti-capital punishment or any controversial cause, will be a definite liability to any candidate.

In political contests there is no clearly recognized code of ethics. Candidates have been stripped of their privacy time after time. Old sins for which atonement has long since been made are dredged up and put on display before the electorate.

Most successful campaign managers of my acquaintance

adhere rigidly to the following rule: All aspects of your opponent's public actions and public statements are fair game. No matter when the action was taken or where a statement was made, you are well within your rights in bringing it to the attention of the voters. A candidate's voting record is public property no matter what sound logic might have provoked the vote at that particular time. *But a man's personal life, the personal life of his family and friends, should never be used.*

If your opponent has been arrested on a drunk driving charge, the arrest is public and the electorate is entitled to know about it. If your opponent has been accused of taking advantage of a partner in a business deal and ultimately was the defendant in a law suit arising from this situation, the electorate is entitled to hear about it. But if your opponent or his wife is a secret alcoholic, if your opponent has a more than platonic relationship with a woman other than his wife, or once associated with disreputable friends, this informations is off limits.

There are politicians whose specialty is the ugly rumor, the derogatory innuendo. Sometimes the electorate is fooled and rewards this kind of filthy action. More often than not such tactics will produce a reaction against the author.

In one California campaign which pitted Will Rogers, Jr. against Bill Knowland for a seat in the United States Senate the Rogers' supporters cried "foul." They said it was a smear when the Knowland camp released proof that Will Rogers, Jr. had written articles for a socialist paper, "The People's Daily World."

But the Democrat candidate had performed a public act; he had at the time of writing been quite willing to have anyone who read the paper see his by-line. When the Knowland forces produced evidence of his one-time association, Mr. Rogers had no legitimate complaint.

Any attack against your opponent which offends the public's sense of fairness will lose votes for your candidate. But when the action or situation exposed has become public property, the cry of "smear" is phony and your candidate will benefit.

If only the public actions of an opponent are fair game for

criticism, what then is the purpose of digging into the non-public history? There are two answers: 1. To protect your own group from making a serious error, and 2. To arm yourself with a real understanding of your opponent's true character.

In one campaign my candidate was running against an entrenched office holder of the opposite party. This man had spent most of his lifetime on the public payroll. His enemies whispered that he had used his political position to acquire three or four thousand acres of valuable farmland.

We hired an aggressive young lawyer and sent him to the title companies. His task was to search out every real estate transaction in which our opponent had figured either as a buyer or a seller. It took him seven weeks to finish the job. His written report was thirty-seven pages long and covered more than that number of separate real estate transfers.

One aspect of the rumor was true—our opponent did hold title to a million dollars worth of land—and it had all been acquired since his first election to public office. But every transaction had been legitimate.

The eager young researcher who brought in the information was confident he had produced the basis for asking some serious questions. "If we go after him on this," he said, "it won't make any difference whether we can prove wrong doing. Just the fact that he owns all this land is enough to make lots of people believe he got it through political deals."

"Yes, they might react in that fashion," I agreed, "but what if they say this just proves that our opponent has sound business judgment?"

So we wasted seven weeks and the thousand dollars it cost us for the agent? Not at all. Later on in that campaign a disgruntled one-time associate of our opponent tried to sell us information which he claimed would insure my candidate's victory. What was the information? A completely false account of how our opponent had connived and cheated to acquire his land holdings. If we had fallen for this tempting offer and made such claims, the reaction would certainly have turned the tide of public support against us. Our painstaking research prevented us from making this error.

It is almost as important to know your true friends as it is to know your enemies. In every campaign there are individuals who want to be with the winner. These people will tell your candidate they are all for him. Ten minutes later they are whispering the same promises of support to your opponent. Special interest groups expect to prosper as the result of political connections. Sometimes they make identical contributions to both candidates. When a contest is close, this class of support is extremely noncommittal. But if research has done its job, the manager will not count on support which doesn't exist and will not be trapped into giving his confidence to individuals who are actually more sympathetic to the opposition. Candidates who like to believe and accept all offers of support as genuine are in desperate need of knowing who their real friends are.

In South Dakota the Rural Electrification Administration publishes the state's most lavish newspaper. The headquarters is knee deep in staff. Many of these executives are capable in the political field. This work is called "Community Relations." It is perfectly legitimate but it does make the REA a real power at election time. Shortly after United States Senator Karl Mundt was elected in 1954 spokesmen for the REA began urging Mundt to soften his opposition toward the expanding bureaucracy of these public power groups.

The second important political factor in South Dakota is the Farmers' Union. Mundt, who had been a severe critic of the federal farm program, a subsidy operation dear to the hearts of the Farmers' Union executives, was courted by representatives of this group.

Every politician wants peace at home. These overtures carried the implication that if Mundt would tone down his criticism—compromise his opposition to an expansion of the REA and the continued farm subsidy—these groups were willing to let bygones be bygones, would offer only a token opposition to his re-election in 1960. The Senator was suspicious of their sincerity, but did not choose to deepen their antagonism. He stood on his record.

The Mundt research organization was slow getting started in 1959. When they finally came in with solid information that the REA and the Farmers' Union had lined up behind Mundt's 1960 opponent, George McGovern, a college professor, the Senator came out swinging. This sudden re-emergence of the old Senator Mundt—a tough-minded, conservative, free enterprise American—so encouraged his followers in South Dakota that he won re-election. But his victory was not certain until twenty-four hours after the polls had closed.

In the 1952 Goldwater Arizona campaign our research revealed that one of the state's most brilliant and successful criminal lawyers was helping to guide the opposition strategy. Our research studies of this individual disclosed a familiar pattern— Attack! Attack! Attack! . . . Challenge a judge . . . Challenge the indictment . . . Challenge the jury. I concluded we could expect a last minute assault on Goldwater.

I couldn't prevent such an attack but I could anticipate it. We bought an additional time segment on the state's only television station for the Monday evening preceding election day. Whatever happened, we would have the last word.

The attack came on the final weekend in a full page newspaper ad and a thirty minute speech on radio. "Goldwater was the spoiled child of a wealthy family. He spent most of his time in La Jolla, California, an exclusive South Coast resort.

"Goldwater was an ingrate. He had in the past solicited and accepted substantial favors from the man he was now trying to defeat."

It was alleged in the attack, although it was untrue, that "Goldwater's war record was pure fabrication."

True or untrue, such charges carry some weight. Goldwater did own a house in California; Goldwater had solicited a favor from his opponent—he had asked the Senator's help in getting a transfer from the Reserves to active duty before the Japs struck at Pearl Harbor.

Goldwater had no combat record. Over-age for such duty at the start of the war, he had out-maneuvered the red tape to get pilot status. Assigned to the Air Transport Command, he had flown in every theatre but the European, but never in combat.

We had twenty-four hours to consider the charges and decide upon a proper course of action. There was a temptation to make an angry answer, to offer overwhelming evidence and refutation of the distorted allegations. We wrote several speeches in this vein. Then we re-read the research report on the man who had made the attack. It was true he had brilliantly defended some notorious offenders. Most of his clients had escaped punishment. He had a small circle of close friends who admired him tremendously. But most of the voters had never seen his name except in connection with some rather notorious evil doer. On the television program Goldwater reviewed the charges without any display of anger or other emotion. Then he said: "I can't understand why this man would say these things about me. I have never shown him anything but kindness."

The job of researching the personalities of the opposition cannot be completed in the normal season of politics. Sometimes the identity of your opponent will not be determined until after mid-summer or early fall primary contests in the opposition party. In such cases facts must be gathered about all the potential opponents, their supporters and probable advisers.

If your candidate is running against an incumbent who is of the opposite party, the Senatorial Campaign Committee and the Congressional Campaign Committee can provide the voting record and a great deal of background information.

In times past purely local elections have taken on national significance. This ususally occurs when one of the candidates is the special champion of a nationwide interest or group. Political units of the AFL-CIO are sometimes sent into a state to assist a candidate who is especially friendly to labor. The public vs. private power controversy has provoked outside participation in what otherwise would be a purely local election. These outside interests frequently contribute significant information to the research file.

In a senatorial contest some years ago industrial interests combined with oil money from Texas to finance a super-duper espionage effort aimed at defeating a candidate who enjoyed the all-out support of organized labor. An out-of-state detective agency, operated by former FBI agents, was hired to produce evidence that out-of-state labor men and money were being used to defeat an incumbent senator. A crew of operators moved into the state. Some of them checked into the hotel where the labor agent was living. They even managed to take the room next door. Everyone who came to see the labor agent was identified. When the agent left his room he was followed and photographed. In some mysterious fashion these sleuths came into possession of a list of telephone calls made by the labor man. They rented the top floor of a downtown office building and a cameraman with a telephoto lens photographed every politician who entered the labor man's hotel.

Such elaborate operations are not always necessary or desirable and they are extremely expensive. The treasurer of this campaign estimated the cost of this one research effort at $37,500. The operation must have been a particularly nerve-wracking one for the manager of that campaign. The presence of out-of-state spies, if disclosed and documented by the opposition, would have been extremely harmful to his candidate. The spies weren't discovered and the shocking disclosures made possible as the result of their efforts helped the candidate to win a resounding victory.

VOTING RECORD

The voting or administrative record of your opponent, depending upon the type of office involved, can always be gathered from public records. But the staff member doing the research must be someone who understands the habits of either the legislative body involved or the administrative office in question.

A "yes" vote on a proposition in the United States House of Representatives or Senate is not always an indication of support for the measure. Parliamentary maneuvers employed sometimes create a situation where "yes" means "no" and "no" means "yes." We discovered this in the '58 Goldwater campaign.

We had been advised that our opponent—one-time Senator Ernest McFarland—had voted "yes" on a particular issue. Goldwater opened that campaign with sharp criticism of McFarland for his "yes" vote. It was a mistake. The Senator had voted "yes" but his affirmative vote was against the bill, not in favor of it. After that experience I personally verified the facts in advance before advising Goldwater to mention any of the McFarland votes.

Such indexes as those prepared by COPE, ADA and the Americans for Constitutional Action are tempting traps for the inexperienced. All of these groups seek to document a particular point of view. Their ratings are based upon selected legislative issues. The total voting record is more informative and a failure to vote, a pair*, or an absence from the chamber can be just as useful as an affirmative or negative action on some measures.

Voters expect their senators and their congressmen to be on hand and to express an opinion on every legislative question. If your opponent is an incumbent, the charge that the senator or the congressman wasn't there when the chips were counted, will cost the absent member dearly at election time.

Issues change, the needs of a constituency change, the state of the economy is never quite the same. Consequently, a position which might have been applauded ten years ago can be a liability today.

* *Members of Congress who find it impossible to be present for an actual vote frequently arrange a 'pair' which links their vote in favor of or against a measure with some other Member of Congress who wishes to vote the opposite way, the result being that each vote is cancelled.*

In the 1958 campaign Goldwater was challenged by the same Democrat he had defeated in 1952. This man had served two terms in the United States Senate and had a voting record.

Beginning in mid-1957 the national economy entered a period of recession. By campaign time the domestic copper mining industry was in serious trouble. Unable to produce at a profit, the mines in Arizona were operating on a part-time basis. Hundreds of miners were out of work. Those fortunate still to have a job were working shortened hours. Three counties were affected—Cochise, Gila and Graham.

Our opponent's itinerary called for personal appearances in Bisbee and Douglas, mining towns where the reduction of the world price of copper had thrown Arizonans out of work.

McFarland had raised the pocketbook issue by claiming the cost of living had gone up under Republicans and that people in Arizona had been better off when he was in the Senate.

We asked our research division to give us what they had on McFarland and copper. There were numerous speeches in the file. In every one our opponent had spoken glowingly about the importance of the copper industry to the economy of Arizona. He was four square in favor of a prosperous mining industry—any other position would have been stupid. Our opponent was not a stupid man.

In 1950, when our opponent had been a member of the United States Senate, there had been a measure before that body calling for the establishment of a four cent protective copper tariff. Democrats don't like protective tariffs and the Truman administration was opposed to this one. Moreover, the copper industry was booming in 1950. Arizona's mines didn't need the four cent advantage. McFarland had voted against establishing peril point protection. At the time there had been no great public criticism of the Senator's position. But if that legislation had been in effect in 1958, it was reasonable to suggest the miners in Bisbee and Douglas would not have been out of work.

We bought all the available radio time we could afford—two minute, three minute and five minute segments. The message was always the same:

"Former Senator McFarland is going to be in Bisbee and Douglas today asking you to vote for him. When McFarland was in the Senate he voted against a four cent peril point protective tariff for copper. If that tariff were in force today, you would probably be on the job instead of being out of work. When the former Senator asks you to vote for him today, why don't you ask him why he didn't vote to protect your job when he had the chance?"

Dirty pool? Not at all. The one-time Senator's vote was a matter of public record. Had the bill passed, the miners would have been working. The fact that the legislation wasn't needed when it was offered had nothing to do with the situation. Its sponsors in that long ago time had urged passage of the measure, not on the grounds that it was needed then, but rather that it might be needed some day and needed desperately.

Was this tactic effective? Goldwater carried Cochise county by 185 votes in 1958. He had lost Cochise County by 2,397 votes in 1952.

When a campaign actually starts it is necessary to have daily information on the activities of the opposition. Someone in research should be assigned to the task of making tape recordings of every radio and television appearance of your opponent. Newspaper statements, stories and advertising must be clipped and kept. Your opponent's itinerary deserves a place on your bulletin board, if for no other reason than to let you know when and where your candidate may come face to face with the opposition. We have found it is best to follow and not to lead. Let the opponent enter the community first but be sure your candidate is not far behind.

Most newspapers have a limit on the space they can devote to politics. When two candidates are in the area the space is divided. When your man comes in after the opposition, he has the upper hand. He can refute any harmful charges made by the opponent. He can raise questions which require an answer, an answer which will be difficult to deliver because it will be physically difficult for the opponent to revisit the scene in time to be effective.

I have heard of spies being planted in an opposition headquarters and I have had people working for the opposition offer to sell me information. A man who will sell out his boss is, in my viewpoint, capable of a double sell-out.

There are many ways of finding out what is going on without employing spies or buying from traitors. One campaign manager of my acquaintance actually made arrangements to receive the contents of the waste baskets from the office of the opposition. He came into possession of carbon copies of letters, envelopes which betrayed the identity of individuals and organizations who had written letters to the opposition, memos in the handwriting of his opponent's manager, telegrams, instructions to the advertising agency and many totally useless items. It took a lot of digging through the trash to come up with the nuggets. But he told me that daily panning produced some very fine gold.

THE ISSUES

Candidates are expected to know the answers. Voters demand that an individual seeking public office be able to discuss and give a reasonable opinion on every subject from grain storage to the conflict over the seals on the Pribilof Islands. No candidate should be expected to know all these things. The world of politics is not a reasonable world.

Every candidate can be rehearsed and be knowledgeable on the principal issues. The method for determining the principal issues is explained in the chapter on Public Opinion Surveys.

Beyond the major questions the candidate is at the mercy of his research organization. If the necessary staff work has been performed efficiently, the candidate can shine in any situation.

This phase of research begins with the compilation of a bibliography. Seek out the authoritative publications on every conceivable subject. Let some staffer make a two or three page digest of what the authors have said. Give two or three opinions if necessary. If the issue is particularly controversial, document opposing positions. This may appear a monumental assignment. In practice we have never found it necessary to build a fact book covering more than 200 issues or situations. By situation I mean such things as the state tax rate over a period of years or federal budget figures or appropriations for government projects in particular categories.

A candidate won't have time to memorize the fact book but he can take it with him. When someone in the audience raises a particular question, the candidate can gracefully acknowledge that he is unwilling to trust his memory on this particular subject, produce the fact book and either read the information or paraphrase it.

I have been present time after time when this kind of a performance earns real Brownie points for the candidate who says: "I just happen to have some information in my brief case on that subject. If you will allow me, I'd like to refresh my memory so that I'll give you accurate information and won't make any mistakes."

It will be helpful when there is a real controversy between your candidate and his opponent to put a few opposition quotes in the fact book. Your candidate can usually give an accurate account of what he has said on a subject. When he then produces and reads what the opposition has said on the very same subject, the differences between the two positions are underscored.

It is in the nature of politics that candidates make statements which they afterward regret. Quote your enemy when you can but be sure you quote him accurately.

The staff members who work daily with the research material can usually provide a manager with what he needs at a particular time. But don't rely on memory, yours or theirs—insist that all of the material be indexed and cross-indexed. A box of three-by-five cards will serve nicely and any librarian can put this information together in such a way as to give the campaign manager the kind of devastating ammunition which will rock the opposition.

Don't use all your fire power at any one time; save some of it for the counterattack and remember that the final two weeks of the campaign are critical. That brave commander at Breed's Hill wasn't thinking of politics when he said: "Don't fire until you see the whites of their eyes." But he might have been.

VOTING HABITS

The fourth general area of research is in the field of the Voting Habits of the Constituency. It is a pure statistical study based upon the history of the past two or three election contests. Because the information developed by this study bears heavily on the problem of where to look for votes, we will deal with it in the next chapter.

8 | Where the Ducks Are

Practical politics is often described as the art of winning elections. Among those who attempt to practice this art there is no greater general misunderstanding than the one which surrounds the title of this chapter.

Over the years I have chosen to describe what will be outlined here as "going where the ducks are." To do this, it is necessary to understand where the ducks will be found. Since all managers and all candidates labor mightily for victory, it would seem the practical necessity of determining the area of greatest probable return would invite the most careful consideration. More often than not candidates devote a great deal of energy and spend substantial sums of money in those areas of the constituency least likely to produce victory.

In the business world a super-salesman is described as one who "can sell fur coats to a South Sea Islander," or "refrigerators to an Eskimo." What is implied in this kind of compliment is a situation where the most unlikely buyer purchases a product he doesn't want and doesn't need.

All too often in the traditional political campaign the candidate expends his energy trying to convince those who are already convinced or to persuade those who are least likely to be persuaded.

In every constituency there are identifiable segments of the population that by tradition consistently favor either the Republican or the Democrat candidate. In recent years big city voters have favored the Democrat candidate. Outside the solid South, rural voters and residents of smaller cities have favored the Republican candidate.

The Democrats have done an extremely effective job of identifying their party as the political instrument which best serves the poor. They have branded the Republicans as the party of the rich and the well to do. This strategem of dividing the electorate on an economic line contains an element of truth. Since the days of Franklin D. Roosevelt, Democrats have invariably supported the welfare state concept. The beneficiaries of the welfare state are at the bottom of the economic ladder. A precinct populated with citizens who are living on unemployment benefits, old age pensions or Aid to Dependent Children checks is not going to be receptive to a Republican candidate whose conscience requires him to suggest that "when the government makes a man dependent, it also robs him of a certain amount of freedom."

There is good evidence to indicate that college graduates earn more money than do those who only graduated from high school. One of the great arguments for higher education is that better schooling leads to better income. The Republican philosophy, which stresses opportunity and responsibility, has a better chance of being understood by college graduates than it does by those with an inadequate education.

Geographical origin has a great deal to do with the voting habits of the population. Southerners are traditionally in the Democrat Party. The War between the States is ancient history but the South has not forgotten about it. The Irish Catholic is apt to vote Democrat. The population in the Mid-West tends to be Republican.

All of these generalizations can be borne out by a study of past voting habits. Yet time after time the green, inexperienced candidate is urged to enter the opposition's strong territory and fight out the election.

I have heard candidates of some experience point to a district or a group of precincts which has traditionally favored the opposition and then declare with great conviction: "I'm going to work those precincts twice as hard as I did in the last campaign."

A precinct that has traditionally given 65 per cent of its vote to a Democrat candidate is obviously composed of voters who either can't hear what the Republican candidates are saying or don't want to hear because of their immutable antagonisms to the Republican Party. A precinct or district that gives 65 per cent of its vote to the Republican Party is obviously composed of Republican-inclined voters who won't or can't listen to the arguments advanced by Democrat candidates. To determine where the ducks are, a candidate must first equip himself with an understanding of where the ducks have been in the past.

The area of greatest probable return will be found in those precincts which your party candidates have carried or lost by five per cent. The fact that in the past a Republican candidate has been able to gather 45 per cent of the vote in a precinct is clear indication that at least 45 per cent of the voters are capable of aligning themselves with the philosophy of a Republican candidate. In such a precinct there will be no traditional or economic barrier to prevent an additional five or six or even ten per cent of the voters from giving their approval to a Republican Party candidate.

In areas where a Republican Party candidate has carried a precinct by five per cent or received 55 per cent of the votes cast, there is good reason to believe that an active campaign will persuade an additional four or five per cent of the voters to give their approval to a Republican Party candidate.

The area of least likely return is to be found in those precincts where in election after election the voters have been almost unanimous in their choice. If 70 per cent or 65 per cent of the votes have gone to a Republican in the past, your Republican candidate will probably be unable to increase that percentage significantly. If 65 per cent or more of the votes have gone to a Democrat candidate in the past, your Republican candidate may persuade an additional two or three per cent to come with him, but the gain will not be substantial.

The season of politics is short. There isn't enough time for every candidate to make a maximum effort in every precinct. But there is always enough time for the candidate to make a maximum effort in the area of greatest probable return.

At the start of any campaign one of the tasks to be assigned to the research department is the compilation of a precinct-by-precinct voting history of the state or constituency. These figures will tell the manager in no uncertain terms where to find the ducks. And the ducks are not flying in the precincts which have overwhelmingly supported your party's candidate in the past or the opposition party's candidate.

In the 1958 Goldwater Arizona election the Senator attended a coffee or a meeting in every precinct which qualified as belonging in the area of greatest possible return. There were many precincts where the Senator didn't make a single appearance. Some of these were predominantly Republican.

Once the manager has determined where the ducks are, he must be prepared to take some abuse in the pursuit of this strategy. There is a fine Republican Legislative District Chairman in Arizona who still cherishes considerable animosity toward me because I insisted Goldwater go after the ducks.

In the final two weeks of the campaign the Senator was scheduled to spend two days in Tucson attending precinct coffees. The evenings were reserved for larger gatherings in legislative districts. Every chairman of a legislative district in the area wanted Goldwater for an evening meeting. One charming lady who was the leader in an area which Republicans traditionally carried by about 65 per cent of the vote insisted she was entitled to the Senator. In an adjacent district candidates in the Republican Party had traditionally lost by about five per cent of the vote. We scheduled the Senator for an appearance in this area.

In 1962, this wonderful partisan chairman of the good district was still criticizing me for my decision. But Goldwater carried that district which other Republicans had lost. The final vote was 51 and a fraction per cent for Goldwater.

In the good Republican district the Senator received precisely the same percentage he and other Republican candidates had enjoyed in the past. We didn't lose anything by not sending him to the good district. We gained six per cent by sending him to what was clearly an area of the greatest probable return.

In the 1960 Curtis election in Nebraska, Dick Spelts and Dick Herman scrupulously followed the practice of sending the Senator into those areas where he could logically expect to make the greatest gains. The Curtis victory in these precincts adds an additional endorsement to the practice of "going where the ducks are."

In the 1960 presidential election, Richard Nixon carried his campaign into every one of the 50 states. He worked just as hard, perhaps harder, in those areas which every knowledgeable Republican recognized as hopeless as he did in those areas which in the past have been favorable to Republican candidates. In the final week of that effort he visited Alaska—an area which could not possibly affect the outcome of the presidential race.

In making the precinct analysis to determine where the ducks are, consideration must be given to the peculiar circumstances of the contest chosen for the index. A more accurate reflection of the voting habits of a precinct will come from a study of two or three contests. Don't choose the stars of any particular year; select some average-to-good candidates in both parties and when the votes have been tabulated, calculate the percentage. The sample sheet on pages 102-103 can be followed as a guide.

In the three precincts shown here for purpose of illustration, we have a four-year history covering three elections and five offices—governor, member of Congress, attorney general, state auditor and state representative.

In 1956, the Republican running for Congress carried Chandler No. 1 precinct. The Republican running for governor lost by a little more than six per cent. The Republican candidate for attorney general lost by 3.39 per cent. The Republican running for auditor lost by 12.93 per cent, but the Republican running for state representative won by 4.89 per cent. This is clearly a potentially profitable precinct for Republican candidates. The 1958 figures demonstrate this conclusively. The Republican candidates for governor, Congress, attorney general and state representative all carried the precinct. In 1958, based on the 1956 performance, this precinct was worth concentrated effort. In 1960, it had forfeited this classification because of the overwhelming '58 Republican vote.

Emerson, the second precinct, shows a steady swing to the Republican candidate; the ducks were here in '56, the hunting was good in '58; and, in 1960, every Republican candidate except the state auditor got more than the limit of birds.

Fowler precinct demonstrates conclusively how the same precinct can switch from party to party. In 1956, the Republican for governor lost, the Republican for the House of Representatives won and the Republicans for attorney general and state auditor were badly defeated. In 1958, the Republican for governor won picking up 9.9 percentage points. The Republican for Congress picked up 3.24 points, but the Republicans for attorney general and auditor both lost ground. In 1960, the Republican for governor again gained, the Republican for Congress lost and the Republican for attorney general gained but not quite enough. It is clear from a statistical point of view, in 1960 the Republican candidate for Congress failed to work the precinct.

When the statisticians have determined the precincts which hold the greatest possibility for your candidate, these should be identified on the voting maps. In most cases a geographical pattern will emerge. The next step is to determine how many votes your candidate must gain or retain in order to win. This becomes your target. If victory can be had by increasing the vote for your party candidate in 50 precincts, concentrate on the 50 which, from your study, offer the greatest possibilities.

The precinct habits can be extremely helpful in determining where the foot soldiers should work, but the best vote-getter on your campaign team is the candidate himself. Schedule coffees, rallies, luncheon club speeches and concentrate them all in the area where past history indicates your candidate will find the audience he needs most.

It would be obvious nonsense to waste your candidate's time in the smaller precincts where a pickup of 10 per cent of the vote might mean a numerical gain of 10 or 20 at the most. Don't ever be tempted to give in to those who urge you to send the candidate into those areas which historically have given 65 or 70 per cent of their votes to the candidate of the opposition party.

There are some strategems that can be employed and that will only be productive when aimed at those who are nominally in the opposition party. But your candidate's time is far too precious to be spent before predominantly hostile audiences. The decision to concentrate on the potentially good areas and neglect the poor ones requires considerable courage on the part of the campaign management. Such a decision will draw the accusation that you are giving up without a fight, that you are conceding certain areas to your opponent; but it isn't rational to try to sell expensive electric refrigerators to impoverished Eskimos when you could be aiming your sales efforts at residents of a warmer climate who are financially able to buy your product.

When the bad or non-productive areas have been identified they should not be abandoned before you ask yourself why. Why is it that these people seem unable to accept your party's candidate? In most cases it will be worthwhile to make a serious effort to understand the thinking of this segment of the voting

PRECINCT VOTE ANALYSIS

Maricopa County, Chandler No. 1 Precinct (Chandler East Precinct Divided in 1958)

YEAR	GOVERNOR			CONGRESS			ATTORNEY GENERAL			AUDITOR			STATE REPRESENTATIVE		
	Dem.	Rep.	% Rep.	Dem.	Rep.	% Rep.	Dem.	Rep.	% Rep.	Dem.	Rep.	% Rep.	Dem.	Rep.	% Rep.
1956	582	457	43.98	444	562	55.86	520	454	46.61	628	370	37.07	452	550	54.89
1958	245	610	71.35	271	568	67.70	380	427	52.91	485	320	39.75	245	601	71.04
1960	407	866	68.03	419	798	65.57	433	812	65.22	669	539	44.62	516	739	58.88

PRECINCT VOTE ANALYSIS

Maricopa County, Emerson Precinct

YEAR	GOVERNOR			CONGRESS			ATTORNEY GENERAL			AUDITOR			STATE REPRESENTATIVE		
	Dem.	Rep.	% Rep.	Dem.	Rep.	% Rep.	Dem.	Rep.	% Rep.	Dem.	Rep.	% Rep.	Dem.	Rep.	% Rep.
1956	487	498	50.55	383	597	60.91	469	497	51.44	556	418	42.91	468	504	51.85
1958	327	533	61.98	343	497	59.17	383	443	53.63	489	329	40.22	432	397	47.88
1960	300	623	67.50	352	536	60.36	352	548	60.89	485	403	45.38	369	495	57.29

PRECINCT VOTE ANALYSIS

Maricopa County, Fowler Precinct

YEAR	GOVERNOR			CONGRESS			ATTORNEY GENERAL			AUDITOR			STATE REPRESENTATIVE		
	Dem.	*Rep.*	*% Rep.*	*Dem.*	*Rep.*	*% Rep.*	*Dem.*	*Rep.*	*% Rep.*	*Dem.*	*Rep.*	*% Rep.*	*Dem.*	*Rep.*	*% Rep.*
1956	141	111	44.04	126	128	50.39	147	96	39.50	181	82	31.17	168	NC	
1958	120	136	53.13	115	133	53.63	153	91	37.30	179	67	27.24	176	77	30.43
1960	152	190	55.56	174	147	45.79	171	160	48.34	238	94	28.31	244	92	27.38

population. A properly conducted public opinion survey may provide the key to your party's lack of popularity and, in some cases, this animosity can be conquered; if not in this election, perhaps in the next one. Managers are concerned with the present election and its outcome, and good managers will "go where the ducks are."

9 | The Cell Group

The military commander who sends his soldiers into battle without having first developed detailed plans for the attack is almost certain to be defeated. The plan of battle must include, among other things, the proper use of specially trained forces as well as the deployment of conventional units.

The troops available in a political campaign are for the most part volunteers. The recruitment, instruction and deployment of volunteer forces is the task of the campaign manager. If he is skillful, his organization will bring sufficient pressure to bear upon public sentiment to produce victory on election day.

The measurable strength of a political party is to be found in its precinct committeemen. In the big urban centers precinct officials frequently benefit from a patronage job. They devote their full time to political work and are paid for it. But outside the big cities the party functionaries are individuals who enjoy the excitement of politics, who derive satisfaction from the recognition they receive as an elected party official. Precinct committeemen choose their own captains, elect legislative district leaders and have a voice in the selection of county and state chairmen. With these people politics is a hobby to which they eagerly devote their leisure time.

Candidates, particularly those for lesser offices, must depend upon the party organization. But a man running for the office of governor, for the U.S. Senate or for Congress needs to establish a private organization. To be successful he must recruit an army of supporters who will give him their first loyalty and devote all of their efforts to advancing his cause.

Precinct organizations get out the party vote. But except in those areas where one party enjoys an overwhelming majority registration, this is not enough to insure victory.

In Arizona, where Democrats outnumber Republicans—the ratio was five to one in 1952 and about three and one half to one in 1958—it would be folly for a Republican candidate to pin his hopes on the regular Republican vote.

Mao Tse-tung, the communist revolutionary general, has written a valuable book on the tactics of infiltration. In it he says: "Give me just two or three men in a village and I will take the village." In the Goldwater campaigns of 1952 and 1958 and in all other campaigns where I have served as a consultant I have followed the advice of Mao Tse-tung.

Almost all candidates try valiantly in one way or another to consolidate their supporters. Politicians steeped in the old tradition frequently organize clubs. Voters are asked to sign up, perhaps contribute a dollar or so, and become a charter member of the "Smith for Senate Club." Frequently these groups are identified by a lapel pin or are given special stickers to put on their cars. The strategy we used is totally different.

For easy identification we called our operation the "Cell Group," because the title suggests precisely what we hoped to create—enthusiastic, knowledgeable Goldwater supporters who would not be labeled or identified as members of any special organization.

The individuals we enlisted became a secret weapon possessing strength, mobility and real impact. They were able to infiltrate centers of opposition support, keep us informed of opposition tactics, disseminate information, enlist other supporters and to do all these things completely unnoticed by the opposition.

As the program is outlined here, it will appear to be simple and the usefulness of such a group will be obvious. My understanding of how to develop such strength and how to use it is the result of trial and error in numerous campaigns. Over the years I have abandoned those techniques which do not produce results.

In those years when I was serving as a special consultant for the Republican Senatorial Campaign Committee I discovered the very simplicity of the plan sometimes made it difficult for the traditional politician to understand the dynamic upon which it operates.

Mao Tse-tung might have been able to take a village with just two or three men. I have learned that to guarantee success in the political effort it is desirable to have three to five per cent of the voting population enlisted in the Cell Group.

In 1958 we finally had about thirty-two hundred Cell Group members in Arizona. In Nebraska in 1960 we had almost one hundred thousand. In this instance the program actually got a little out of hand. In Massachusetts, Chuck Colson, a director of the 1960 campaign for Senator Saltonstall, kept the membership in his Cell Group within manageable limits.

Before we examine the mechanics of enlisting Cell Group members, it will be helpful to review the considerations that prompt individuals to volunteer for any service outside the narrow orbit of their everyday lives.

Volunteers in a political effort do not expect to receive any direct financial or material return from their work. The appeal to them must be essentially an emotional one. To be successful it must contain something more than the oft repeated request of a candidate for a voter's support. The plan outlined in this chapter suggests involvement, an entering into the inner circle, with access to information not available to the general public.

The foundation of a successful Cell Group organization requires a wide acquaintance with the individuals in the constituency. It isn't at all necessary that the individuals selected be close friends of the candidate.

As the first step the candidate is asked to list the names of important or competent individuals with whom he is acquainted. It is helpful to indicate the actual relationship by establishing three categories: close personal friends, close political associates, individuals who are known to the candidate but not necessarily on a personal basis.

In setting up the file we used three different colored cards to indicate the categories. On a large list the use of IBM equipment is almost mandatory. To gain the maximum return from the Cell Group operation it is necessary to be able to identify the Cell Group members by occupation, economic status and geographical location.

An incumbent politician will have no difficulty providing an adequate number of names in all three groups. Men in public office have a wide circle of personal friends. The practicing politician establishes contacts with people who are not necessarily close friends on the basis of mutual interest.

The incumbent's correspondence file can provide the names of individuals in every community who have been sufficiently interested in the problems of government to write him one or more letters during his tenure in office.

An individual who is a candidate for the first time may have more difficulty with the names. But if a man can be considered a serious candidate for a public office, he must enjoy a wide acquaintance. The first-timer will probably fill his list with the names of business associates, service club or church contacts, or members of the party if he has been active in politics.

The candidate's manager and those who are to be closely associated with the campaign effort can very likely contribute as many useful names as the candidate himself. The manager must give balance to the list. I dislike the odious term "little people" but that phrase best illustrates what I mean by balance.

A candidate will know the big shots; the managers must add names to make the total list representative as nearly as possible of the total constituency.

When the list has ben compiled, the research division—an activity discussed in another chapter—should provide as much additional information as possible. It will be helpful to know the financial situation of the respective Cell Group member, his banking connection, his relationship with the home town newspaper, his church or lodge identification, his occupation or profession, and his family connections throughout the state. If the individual has been active in politics, this information will be extremely important. The quality of the individuals suggested is much more important than the quantity. As the campaign progresses the list will grow.

The initial approach should be made with a personal letter—from the candidate if the candidate supplied the name or from the manager or associate who put the name on the list.

The whole problem of the use of mail in a political campaign will be discussed in depth in another chapter. For our purpose at this moment, however, it is necessary to understand the kind of first letter that will produce a favorable response.

The objective is to cement the relationship between the recipient of the letter and the candidate. Ultimately we want to establish a mutual interest and to develop this interest to such a degree that the member of the Cell Group will be strongly identified with the candidate's fortunes, will actually come to consider the threat of defeat as menacing him personally.

The approach must be on a first-name basis. If no one in the campaign group knows the individual well enough to call him by his first name, put that card aside for future development. The letter must be personally typed, not reproduced—robotyped letters have the appearance of being individually typed but the uniformity or similarity of the contents of such letters makes it dangerous to take this short-cut in the initial approach. It can be assumed that a number of the individuals selected for enlistment in this Cell Group will share some mutual interest; they might be close friends. Since anyone approached with the kind of letter we have in mind will be both pleased and flattered, the danger that one of the recipients might show his letter to someone who has also been approached is a risk that must not be taken at this time.

The content of all the letters—whether written by the candidate or by his associates—is basically an appeal for the opinion or the judgment of the individual addressed. NOTHING IS SAID WHICH WOULD INDICATE THAT THE REAL INTENT OF THE LETTER IS TO INVOLVE THE RECIPIENT IN A POLITICAL CAMPAIGN.

The reason for the letter must be clear in the very first paragraph. Assuming the candidate's name is Robert Maxwell:

> Dear Jim:
>
> The Banking and Insurance Committee of the Senate is considering HB-146. The sponsors of this bill claim it will give more protection to a bank's depositors. If you could take time to read the enclosed copy of this proposed legislation and let me have the benefit of your thinking, I would be most grateful.
>
> Some of our staff members will work up information on the proposal but I feel the need of your knowledge and your understanding. A long time ago, Jim, I learned that the people back here don't always think the same way as the people in Arizona.
>
> > Gratefully yours,
> > Bob

Why does the letter lead off with the discussion of legislation affecting banking? Because the research division has provided the information that Jim is a stockholder in a bank or a board member or an attorney in a firm which represents banking interests.

In each session the Congress considers a wide variety of proposed new legislation. It is never difficult to find a particular bill which will lie in the special area of competence belonging to the individual to whom the letter is being written.

If the letter is to be written by someone other than the candidate, it might go like this:

> Dear Jim:
>
> When Bob was here last week, (if the Senator hadn't been in the state, the letter might begin: "I was talking with Bob on the telephone last week.") he mentioned he was concerned with some legislation which is being considered by the Banking and Currency Committee. It has to do with new regulations being offered as additional protection for bank depositors.
>
> Bob would be very interested in having your opinion on the subject.
>
> I am enclosing a copy of the proposed legislation. If you want to send your opinion direct to me, I will forward it on to Bob. But better still, just address your letter to him at the Senate Office Building in Washington, D. C.

(At this point, if the author of the letter is someone other than the candidate, there is an opportunity for a comment on the local political situation.) For example:

> We hear that a good deal of Eastern labor money will come into the state to beat Bob Maxwell next year. It's going to be a real battle.
>
> Gratefully yours,
> Steve

A request for advice or an opinion on proposed legislation provides an incumbent with a logical and legitimate reason for the letter. The resourceful campaign manager can find dozens of other reasons for writing just as valid—an editorial from a newspaper, a reprint from a magazine which the Senator believes the constituent would enjoy reading, an impending action by the administration.

In December of 1963 Secretary of Defense McNamara announced the closing of a great many military installations throughout the country. In those areas affected there was an immediate editorial reaction. A candidate seeking election to the

Congress would find this an ideal springboard for the first letter. The communication would contain a reproduction of the editorial and then solicit the individual's opinion as to the effect the proposed action would have on the community.

There are a number of very sound reasons why the initial approach should seek an opinion from the recipient. Anyone is flattered when a U.S. Senator or a man of sufficient stature to be a logical candidate for the U.S. Senate asks his advice. When the form of advice solicited calls on the individual's special field of competence, the implication of respect is even stronger.

The candidate may find some very useful opinions in the responses. The real benefit from the request is that it requires the individual to act. This action is the forerunner of a real commitment. In this trade of managing campaigns which I have followed for so many years, we call it accountability. Ask somebody to do something for you. Make the request flattering if possible. Provide the necessity for positive action. And wherever practical put a deadline on the response.

In those letters that have as their subject proposed legislative action, there is an implicit deadline. The committee is holding hearings, therefore the Senator needs a response before the legislation is brought before the Senate for action. If the excuse for the letter is a proposed governmental action, a response is required before the action becomes final.

The recruitment of Cell Group members is a gradual process. At the outset the tempo will be limited by the clerical help available to the candidate or his manager. Because the letters are personalized and suited to fit the special interest or ability of the recipient, it will be difficult to send out more than a hundred a day. The manager must keep enough clerical help in reserve to respond promptly to the answers as they come in. An immediate reply to the return letter is essential to the ultimate organization of an effective Cell Group.

The acknowledgment must be a personal letter. It must be directly responsive to the suggestions made by the citizen, but it should do much more than express thanks or gratitude. The tone of the second letter assumes a continuing relationship.

This original approach and first response, requiring individually typed letters and first class postage, is the most expensive part of the Cell Group operation. The exchange of letters on a personal basis is continued for only a very short time. In some campaigns we have moved names to a general bulk mailing list after the first exchange. Sometimes, owing to the nature of the response or the prominence of the individual involved, this correspondence has been continued on a personal basis for some little time. But the objective is to have all the names on a single bulk mailing list, receiving duplicated letters as soon as possible.

If the approach has been carried out with some skill and sensitivity, the transition to bulk mailing will not be resented. A high degree of skill is required in the preparation and wording of the mass communications. Mailings must not be sent with any kind of calendar regularity. The letter or other material in the communication must document and explain the reason for the letter. Never at any time should there be an indication that the recipient is a member of an organized group.

In all my experience I have had only one angry objection to the use of duplicated letters sent to a Cell Group. This came about because the recipient resented the fact that my name was signed to the letter rather than the candidate's.

In developing this technique I made a serious effort to interview Cell Group members after election day. I learned their interest was in the content of the communication. The form went almost unnoticed. Some of them told me they realized others were getting the same information or, as they put it, "I knew Barry was sending this stuff to some of his good friends but most of the people I talked to weren't getting it and I was real pleased to be a part of the inner circle."

Once the initial contact has been established, the campaign manager will have no difficulty in finding a valid reason for further letters. Editorials from an out of state newspaper, reprints from the Congressional Record, a copy of a letter the candidate has sent to someone setting forth his position on an issue and finally, advance information on the candidate's plans.

Many individuals enlisted in the Cell Group will respond by asking: "What can I do to help?" At this point the manager is in a delightful position. It is a real advantage to have someone ask: "What can I do?" Because the suggestions made in response to that request rarely arouse any antagonism. None of us really like to be told what to do. When a manager sends out a suggestion cold he can be sure someone will make an angry response.

The list of things Cell Group members can do for a candidate is almost inexhaustible. They can provide an accurate index to public sentiment as participants in the continuous survey—a technique fully described in the chapter on public opinion polls. They can and will keep the manager constantly advised on activities of the opposition.

In 1958 we had Cell Group members working for most of the radio and television outlets in Arizona. We were informed immediately when the opposition tripled its request for time on the Saturday, Sunday and Monday immediately preceding election day. This told us in advance the opposition was coming up with some new tactic, some new appeal, and we were able to turn the sudden flood of buy orders into an ultimate liability for our opponent.

The most important service performed by the Cell Group members is to mention the name of your candidate favorably to everyone they meet.

In 1948 the University of Chicago sponsored an investigation into the voting habits of the people of Elmira, New York. This city was selected, after careful study, as being typical. Information was developed through a series of interviews commencing in June and concluding after election day. The sample selected was carefully weighted to represent a true cross section of the socio-economic divisions of the population. In discussing the August to November voting changes, the authors reveal that nine per cent of one group changed to the opposite party candidate sometime before election day. This nine per cent who intended to vote for Dewey in June but switched to Truman in November, or vice versa, made the change because they had a majority of friends who were opposed to their June decision. A nine per cent switch can change the outcome of any election.

The surveys in Elmira also revealed that twenty-five per cent of those who had family members in the opposite party switched from their intended choice in June to their family's choice in November. For the purpose of understanding and then exploiting those voters whose minds can be changed, it is important to emphasize that this substantial switch was brought about through personal contact and family pressures.

The members of a "Smith for Senate Club" of the old tradition were all identified partisans. Their endorsement of Smith loses much of its strength because of their identification with an organized group pushing Smith.

The members of the Cell Groups are not publicly identified as partisans in the same sense prominent party members or members of a candidate club are identified. The opinions of the Cell Group members are more readily accepted because their endorsement does not carry the same implication of self-service which is attached to a party official, or to a publicly identified member of a partisan club. Cell Group members can be recruited from both major parties and when a man who is nominally Democrat, who in past elections has publicly supported candidates on the Democrat ticket, advances the cause of a Republican candidate, his words carry real conviction.

The Cell Groups have a second advantage over the traditional clubs, for such clubs draw together like-minded people and members of such clubs are inclined to associate with each other rather than spreading out. A Cell Group member, on the contrary, frequently finds himself in company with members of the opposition. His social activity is not limited to individuals with strong political convictions.

Of course a citizen who wanders about saying: "Senator Smith's a wonderful guy. I hope you'll vote for him" will immediately be identified as a partisan and soon rejected as a bore with a one-track mind. It is up to the manager to use his Cell Group members effectively. He must keep them from being robot partisans. The campaign manager must use his mass mailings to keep the individuals in this group supplied with a valid reason for injecting the candidate's name into every conversation. His job is to supply the Cell Group with inside information which will in turn become a natural point of departure for injecting the candidate's name into every conversation.

We all like to talk about things in our particular field of special knowledge or special competency. If we read a book or see a new play, the book or the play becomes our topic of conversation for a few days. If we know something about a public figure that is not general knowledge, we are eager to display the fact that we have access to inside information.

If the candidate is going to make a speech on an important subject, the speech should be duplicated well in advance in order that it may be distributed in advance. The first page should be marked: "Not for release until . . . (the date the speech is to be delivered)." Copies are mailed to members of the Cell Group together with a letter something like this:

> Bob is going to speak on Federal Aid to Education in Lincoln on such and such a date. He thought you would like to know in advance what he is going to say. Please keep this matter confidential until after the release date.

Now the members of the Cell Group are really on the inside. They have the speech ahead of the newspapers; the candidate has trusted them with this confidential information. They will find it impossible to resist the temptation to talk about it.

Some members of the Cell Group will quote directly from the speech. But most of them, mindful of the situation, will confine their remarks to something like this: "The Senator is going to make a speech two weeks from now. He's got a lot to say and it's about time someone said it."

With that kind of a starter the conversation is really opened. It is centered on the candidate. The Cell Group member has been provided with the most logical reason to talk about his favorite politician.

I have learned that just sending the candidate's itinerary to members of the Cell Group is beneficial. If the candidate is going to make a speech or is appearing in some section of the state three hundred miles away, the Cell Group member knows it. He can and will inject the candidate's name into the conversation quite naturally by mentioning where the candidate is going to be.

The utility of the Cell Group does not end with its ability to spread the word about the candidate. It can be used to counterattack the opposition in a dozen different ways.

In the election described in an earlier chapter, Senator —————————was defeated in part through the circulation of a derogatory rumor. Had his managers established a Cell Group in that state, they might very well have destroyed the effectiveness of that slander.

The campaign manager is required to develop an intimate knowledge of his opposition. This is discussed at length in the chapter entitled *Researching the Opposition* but to understand how the Cell Group organization can protect a candidate, the subject must be mentioned briefly here.

The security surrounding campaign headquarters can be penetrated. Knowing in advance what the opposition proposes is very useful information indeed. Acquaintance with the habits of the men leading the opposition will permit the campaign manager to prepare a defensive counterattack—something to be held in readiness until it is needed.

In 1958 in Arizona, at the outset of the campaign, I learned that among our opponent's camp followers was an individual whose forte was the circulation of harmful rumors.

Armed with this information, I immediately sent a communiqué to all Cell Group members. In it I explained the probability that someone, somewhere, would start an ugly rumor about Goldwater. To give them an idea of what I anticipated, I recited the history of the————————campaign. Then I asked the Cell Group members to report by telephone the moment they encountered this tactic in their community.

From certain sources extremely antagonistic to Goldwater, we heard the charge that his department store paid substandard wages. Our intelligence produced the information that an employee in the Goldwater store had been approached and questioned about her salary. The conversations had culminated with the Goldwater clerk selling her paycheck to those who made the inquiry. It seemed necessary to anticipate a rumor attacking Goldwater as a rich man who paid substandard wages.

In preparing to combat this possibility, we decided the best testimony to refute such a charge would be a statement from Goldwater employees and we prepared a full page newspaper ad. [Note: This kind of appeal will be discussed in detail in the chapter on Mass Media.] The burden of the message was: "We, the undersigned employees of the Goldwater store, receive wages above average for department stores in the Phoenix area. We enjoy benefits not available from other managements. We deeply resent any suggestion that we are to be pitied or that the Goldwater management in any way mistreats us."

Such an ad could not be used in the ordinary course of the campaign because it would appear too self-serving. We believed it would be most effective in response to a rumor alleging Goldwater paid substandard wages. We intended to time the response to the appearance of the rumor.

On a particular day in August we received more than thirty telephone reports from members of the Cell Group residing in every geographical area in the state. The rumor that Goldwater paid low wages was heard almost simultaneously in Yuma and Douglas. These communities are almost three hundred miles apart. The rumor was documented or based on the experience of a supposed relative and quoted the net amount of a paycheck after deductions. And the language of the rumor started in Douglas was identical with the language employed in Yuma:

"My brother's wife works at the Goldwater store. I just couldn't believe it when she told us her paycheck for two weeks work was only XXX dollars."

Having anticipated this attack in advance, I was able to quote the gross amount paid by the Goldwater store to employees in several categories. I told the Cell Group members who called to ask the rumor spreaders if they were talking about gross or net pay and to suggest if their brother's wife received only XXX dollars, she must be a part-time employee.

Seventy-two hours after the story was started our full page advertisement appeared in the state's major newspapers. The message of the ad was strengthened by the fact that space for its display was purchased and paid for by Goldwater employees, not by the Goldwater campaign group.

In that '58 campaign the officials of organized labor were all out to beat Goldwater. They refused to sell us space in the labor publication; they refused to give Goldwater an audience at labor meetings. Our strategy was to try to reach the men who worked with the tools.

One Tuesday afternoon in the middle of that campaign summer I received a telephone call from a Cell Group member. This man, a registered Democrat, was a member of an important union. He called to report that his group was holding a regional meeting in a community one hundred and fifty miles from Phoenix. He said the official agenda was a short one. He had asked union officials if Goldwater could appear and had been refused but he had an idea:

"There's a vacant storeroom next to our union hall. If we could get that storeroom and have Barry there making a speech, I think most of the boys would drift in to hear him."

It was a good suggestion. Could we implement it? In the card file we had about sixty-five names of Cell Group members in this community.

Thanks to the background material supplied by the research division we were able to locate a member who was a real estate man. It developed this member represented the owner of the vacant storeroom.

I didn't have to leave Phoenix. I called each member of the Cell Group in that city and explained our problem. In less than twenty-four hours they were able to do these things: secure the use of the vacant store building without charge; borrow and install portable air conditioning equipment; borrow and install one hundred and fifty folding chairs. They painted signs on the window advertising the meeting. They put spot announcements on their radio station inviting people to come to the meeting. They organized a refreshment committee to provide lemonade, soft drinks, cookies, and I am told there was beer in the back room—but I never asked about that. They produced a nucleus of the audience. That night, by actual count, Goldwater spoke to seventy-six members of the labor union.

Tucson, Arizona, is a delightful, sophisticated, winter resort city, home of the University of Arizona. Its buildings are reminiscent of the Spanish occupation, but the barber shop conversations are typical of the rest of America—sports, politics, the day's news.

The owner of one barbershop in Tucson was a most enthusiastic and effective member of our Cell Group. We didn't find him—he found us. Many months before the actual campaign commenced, he had written me asking for a photograph of the Senator.

In the spring of 1958, the Congress was going through its perennial hassle over foreign aid. As one of our bits of inside information, we had sent to all Cell Group members a brief résumé of committee action on the foreign aid bill together with Goldwater's remarks on the subject.

The week our barber friend received this information he entertained as his customer a prominent citizen long identified with the Democrat cause. This man had been a major contributor to Governor McFarland's Democrat campaign in 1956. He had just returned from a trip around the world—a trip which had taken him into Southeast Asia. He was in the process of being shaved when he mentioned that he had landed at an airport in some far away little country with so many magnificent buildings and so many runways it made the Los Angeles Municipal Airport look like a cow pasture operation.

Our barber friend responded by saying, "Did you read what Barry Goldwater has to say about the waste in foreign aid?"

The traveler expressed interest.

"He sent me a copy of his speech along with some other information on what they are proposing to do about foreign aid," the barber said.

"Where is it?"

"I've got it right here."

"Let me see it."

The traveler sat up in the chair and while the lather dried on his face he carefully read Goldwater's comments. Then he said, "Well, I never voted for a Republican before, but I'll be damned if I'm not going to do it this time."

He did more than vote. He contributed over $3500 to Goldwater's campaign and was probably personally responsible for the votes of at least one hundred Democrats who followed him across the party line.

All of this might have happened anyway because the individual involved was intelligent, was offended by the foreign aid situation, and took more than a passing interest in politics. We think the fact that a barber came up with the right supporting information at exactly the right time was the key in this switching of support.

Members of a Cell Group can be useful in many other ways. They can prepare a climate of disbelief by suggesting in their everyday conversations that "your opponent will probably follow a certain course of action or make certain declarations." By predicting the future action of the opposition, it is possible to turn what might be a liability into an asset.

In the early spring of 1962 prospects for a Republican victory in a number of congressional races were bright indeed. The Kennedy administration was suffering because people were blaming the President for his failure to take decisive action in regard to communist Cuba.

By mid-summer it seemed obvious the administration would have to take some positive act to quiet the criticism and to rehabilitate Kennedy's position in this regard. A few candidates in races across the country timidly advised the voters to expect some such action. But to my knowledge there was no well organized effort to attack in advance the credibility of any dramatic last-minute gesture in regard to Cuba.

In Oregon, where a good Republican candidate, Sig Unander, was challenging Wayne Morse, the polls showed Unander gaining in October and gaining at a rate which, if continued to election day, would bring about a defeat of Morse.

When President Kennedy dramatically challenged Premier Khrushchev and ordered the removal of missiles from Cuba, Unander started to slide and Morse began to gain.

The Kennedy managers had timed their operation perfectly. Senator Keating and others had been warning of the Russian build-up in Cuba since early in the spring of 1962. It is difficult to believe that a single Senator had access to more reliable information than was available to the administration. But a move to halt the build-up of Russian strength in Cuba in May or June would have lost some of its impact by November.

It is my opinion that if Sig Unander had developed a well organized Cell Group in Oregon, he could have disseminated Senator Keating's warning, coupled with a prediction to expect dramatic action and taken the edge off the administration's last-minute maneuver.

In that election contest the voters in Oregon supported a Republican for governor but sent Democrat Morse back to the United States Senate. This demonstrates that enough voters in Oregon crossed the party line in 1962 to have made victory possible for Unander. The Oregon voters simply responded to a magnificent political maneuver, to the kind of stimulation that a campaign manager cannot generate completely independent of events, but a stimulus that can be cleverly exploited.

10 | The Foot Soldiers

The complexion of the electorate will vary slightly from state to state but the difference is never more than one of degree. There may be more committed voters in one constituency than in another—there are always enough Indifferents and Undecideds to turn the tide in an election contest.

The campaign manager who understands the make-up of the electorate and what is required to motivate a favorable action will always attempt to arouse the Indifferents.

The candidate must inspire the party faithful; he must radiate confidence; he must challenge the opposition; he must please his audience. All this is quite an undertaking. The voter who has seen him personally or heard him speak is more likely to be influenced by that brief personal contact than he is by advertising or literature. But in most constituencies it is physically impossible for a candidate to appear in person before, or to be seen by, more than an insignificant number of the voting population.

Television has increased the opportunities for personal confrontation. Skillful use of this new medium may one day revolutionize the whole field of politics. The candidate may be charming on TV. He may be extremely persuasive. But the members of the indifferent group will most likely be watching

"Rawhide" or "Perry Mason" when the candidate is on the channel discussing those issues that will affect the direction of the world.

The mathematics of majority decision are irrefutable. The Indifferents and the Undecideds must be reached; they must be persuaded to vote for your candidate.

When I began managing political campaigns in Arizona in 1938 it was possible for a candidate to meet and shake hands with a high percentage of those who would be qualified to vote for him. Traditional politicians still put great faith in the personal handshake, the quick greeting, the plea: "I hope you'll vote for me."

The candidate's personal appeal for support can be multiplied effectively through the proper use of an especially enlisted group of supporters. These are the foot soldiers. They walk the streets in their own neighborhoods and ask for votes. They do this on a person-to-person basis. They become the candidate's private army, mobilized to do a particular job at a certain time. In my experience a candidate with a properly enlisted group of foot soldiers has never failed to win election.

The purpose of a political campaign can be summed up in one sentence—to address a persuasive request to every registered voter to support your candidate at the polls.

The foot-soldier program is designed to implement that sentence. Because the Indifferents *are* indifferent, the approach to them must be made on a personal basis if that is possible. Some campaign devices or strategies gain their maximum effect by being widely publicized. Having an overflow crowd on hand when the candidate appears indicates popularity and strength. Prominent citizens who declare their support for your candidate attract those who like to follow the leader.

The foot-soldier campaign is particularly effective because it can be organized and used quietly. Usually when the opposition does discover what is going on, it is too late to make an effective counterthrust.

The program permits the enlistment and deployment of a substantial number of workers for an extremely modest allocation of campaign funds. The foot-soldier campaign exerts its maximum influence just before decision day. A similar effort by the opposition might minimize the effect of your foot soldiers; it cannot cancel out their efforts.

The concept is simple; the results obtained are magnificent. It is difficult to understand why the foot-soldier program outlined here or some variation on this theme is not employed by every candidate. The only comparable operation I have ever observed is the almost traditional use of precinct workers to get out the vote on election day.

Many voters complain of the ho-hum deadly similarity between all political campaigns. As the day of decision approaches the differences between the candidates have been clearly defined. The superior virtues of candidate Jones have been spelled out in the newspapers. Jones has been on the radio and on the television asking his fellow citizens to vote for him.

Jones can't knock on every door. It is physically impossible for him to say in person to every voter: "Please vote for me." The next best thing is to send someone to knock on that door on behalf of Jones. If the emissary selected carries the credentials of a neighbor who believes in Jones, who because of this belief is asking *his* neighbor to vote for Jones, the response will be amazing.

"Such a request wouldn't influence me," says a committed member of the Democrat Party, "I know who I'm going to vote for."

"My own mother couldn't change my mind," says the active Republican.

The foot-soldier program isn't calculated to influence anyone who has a firm political conviction. Great caution must be exerted not to stir up political arguments. The foot soldiers are not commissioned to try to convince by logic. Their single assignment is to say: "Mr. Jones is a good man. Please vote for Mr. Jones."

In our complex urbanized society we may not know the name of the man who lives four houses down the street. But if he comes to our door and identifies himself as the man *who lives four houses down the street,* there is an immediate bond between us because we are neighbors. This is the key to the success of the program—the man asking you to vote for Mr. Jones is your neighbor. It is impossible to treat him as a stranger.

In most residential areas such a call would be made under more favorable conditions. If the householders have children in the same school, the chances are good the caller's name will be known. In most cases the caller will not be a stranger. The common concern and mutual interests of people who live in the same neighborhood argues in favor of the foot soldier program.

Voters living in the same geographical area shop at the same neighborhood grocery store, patronize the same cleaner, buy milk from the same dairy. They may go to the same church or have youngsters in the same Boy Scout troop.

In our lonely society all of us hunger for identification. Most of us instinctively resist the impersonal association. In any crowd we seek to find a familiar face. We want to belong to the group. We feel closest to our own family members. Next we cling to early friendships. But with the exception of the completely dehumanized, stratified society, we respond warmly to the claims of our neighbors.

The foot-soldier program has other aspects to recommend it. People who can be solicited to work for a political candidate are more apt to be extrovert than introvert. The shy and the retiring cannot be drawn into an activist political effort. Usually the people who respond to an appeal for campaign workers are the same people who have been enlisted to make calls for United Fund or the Cancer Society or the Red Cross or the

Boy Scouts. This increases the likelihood of their names being known and enhances their credentials as neighbors.

If the solicitor has been instructed properly, he cannot possibly arouse any antagonism. If the person called upon is not strongly committed to one candidate, this personal plea for his vote from a neighbor may be the only truly compelling reason he will have to make a choice between the candidates on election day.

Every successful sales manager instructs his new recruits in this fashion: if you work hard and make enough calls, if you ask enough people to buy, you won't have to worry about making enough sales.

The foot-soldier program, properly organized, will completely blanket a residential area. The plea on behalf of your candidate will be delivered in person to every qualified voter in the precinct or the district.

The size of the task force required for this personal solicitation will vary with the population of the constituency. In the Arizona Goldwater campaign of 1958 we had a few more than 7,000 foot soldiers working their neighborhoods on behalf of Goldwater. In Douglas County, Nebraska, in the Curtis campaign of 1960, Dick Herman had about 3,400 foot soldiers calling for Senator Carl Curtis. In the 1962 Senatorial campaign in Utah, Tom Judd had about 8,000 asking neighbors to support Senator Wallace F. Bennett.

Canvassers are asked to cover the houses on their side of the street in their block. They are instructed not to engage in arguments; not to discuss their candidate in contrast to his opponent. Their task is to knock on the door of their neighbor's home, hand out a piece of especially prepared literature and as a *neighbor* ask their *neighbor* to vote for the candidate.

People who respond to an appeal for volunteer workers always intend to carry out their commitment. The campaign manager must help them avoid the great temptation to procrastinate. The instructions are to make the calls sometime in the five-day period before election day. This deadline is helpful but to inject a still further element of accountability, we have always included a postal report card in the packet of literature distributed to the workers.

The number of houses to a block will vary. In the 1958 Goldwater campaign we estimated that our 7,000 neighbors made an average of eight calls each. 56,000 pieces of literature were distributed in the five-day period before Election Tuesday. If 70 per cent of those contacted were committed voters, we still reached 16,800 who might have been undecided or indifferent.

If each canvasser secured an average of only one favorable vote, the total is still impressive: 7,000 neighbors votes, plus the certain vote of the worker, amounts to 14,000 votes for Goldwater in an election which was won by a majority of only 35,000. Almost one-half of this victory could have been produced by this single volunter effort.

When the project was first started I questioned seriously our ability to enlist enough volunteers to make the house calls. When the volunteers had actually been enlisted and the literature was being prepared for distribution, I was still skeptical. The instruction sheet with each packet suggested that when the canvassing had been completed, the worker should estimate whether the response was favorable or unfavorable and forward to us his opinion on the postal report card. But I was impatient.

The third day after the packets of literature had been delivered I selected a list of volunteers at random. I limited my choice to those precincts which by tradition had gone overwhelmingly to the Democrat Party candidate. One of these precincts surrounds the State Capitol. The homes are modest but well cared for. Many of the people in the neighborhood work for the state government in various capacities. Goldwater's opponent was the incumbent Democrat governor.

When I set out to call on the volunteers to get their personal reaction, I was still unconvinced the device would be successful. At my first stop I introduced myself to an extremely articulate member of a minority group. I told him I wasn't trying to find out which of his neighbors were going to vote for Goldwater. I just wanted to know what the general reaction had been.

"Very good, very good," he said, "most of the people I talked to on this block are going to vote for Barry."

Partisans are frequently incapable of objective judgment. Obviously this man wanted Goldwater to win. The thought flashed through my mind that perhaps I was being told something the volunteer thought I wanted to hear.

I made seven more calls before lunch. In every case the reaction was the same. One dear lady responded to my question in a whisper: "Oh, I can't tell you how my neighbors are going to vote. They all work down there for Mr. McFarland," she said, nodding toward the Capitol, "but you tell Mr. Goldwater it's all right."

It was all right. We carried a number of very doubtful precincts and got a much higher vote in the rest of them than any Republican had ever enjoyed before. I was convinced.

The foot soldiers are all recruited on the telephone. To implement this neighbor-calling-on-neighbor campaign the first step is to get an accurate map of the area to be covered. Count the blocks. This will give you the number of volunteers needed and will determine the number of telephones required. I use the word *telephones* rather than *telephone callers* because it is impossible for one girl to work constantly eight hours a day.

If the map reveals there are 5,000 blocks to be covered, 5,000 canvassers will be required. One telephone can solicit approximately thirty canvassers per day. Thirty divided into 5,000 is 166.6—the number of days it would take to solicit the needed workers with one telephone.

If the manager elects to allocate twenty calling days to enlist his workers, he will need 8.3 telephones. To be safe he should order ten and then man the telephone room with fifteen experienced operators and at least three supervisors. Working twenty or thirty minute shifts, the girls will retain their charm and poise no matter how many "not at homes" or wrong numbers they encounter. And your telephone girl's voice must be warm, friendly and cheerful. We have always used professional operators and paid them for the work.

Volunteers can look up names and telephone numbers, bring coffee and assemble and deliver packets. Preparing the list of names to be called will usually take longer then the actual calling and this work can be commenced thirty or forty days before the telephones are put to work.

The operators must be carefully trained—cautioned never to depart from the established solicitation speech. Professional operators will complete their calls in the time allotted. They will refrain from engaging in any conversation not indicated. They can be counted upon to retreat gracefully without offending if the request for help is refused.

The request, to be successful, must be made in the name of the candidate.

"Mrs. Jones, this is Mary Brown. (The telephone operator should use her correct name.) I'm calling for Senator Robert Maxwell. Would you be willing to help in his campaign for re-election?"

Another form which has worked well for us:

"Mrs. Jones, this is Nina Gleeson. I'm calling for Senator Robert Maxwell. He asked me to *ask you* to help him in his campaign. Would you be willing to do that for him?"

If the person called expresses annoyance, reluctance, or indicates a non-receptive attitude, the call is terminated. If the person called indicates a desire to comply with the Senator's request but expresses inability to do so, the operator says: "Mrs. Jones, I know Senator Maxwell will understand. Thank you very much."

The type of response from each person called should be recorded on the name and number list. If it is hostile, there is a chance the party precinct worker might be able to iron out the difficulty. If it is warm and friendly but for some valid reason a non-volunteer, the name should go to the precinct organization or to whoever is responsible for getting out the favorable votes.

If the person called is receptive and asks what he or she can do to help the candidate, the operator replies: "Bob wants you to call on your neighbors . . . just the people who live in your block on your side of the street . . . and ask them to vote for him. Could you do that, Mrs. Jones?"

If the response is affirmative, further instructions are given: "Thank you very much, Mrs. Jones. We will deliver a packet of literature to your house on such-and-such a date. (This should be the Tuesday before election day.) Your packet will contain your identification, a letter of instruction and a little pamphlet about Maxwell. What he wants you to do is to visit the neighbors in your block. Bob knows that when you tell your neighbors you are going to vote for him and ask them to vote for him, it will really help."

There may be another thirty seconds of conversation before the operator can conclude with: "Bob will be very pleased and very grateful when I tell him you are going to help us, Mrs. Jones. Thank you."

In some cases it may be impossible to enlist a recruit in every block. When this happens it is necessary to ask someone to travel a block or two from his own home to make the calls. But the volunteers must be recruited from an adjacent street if they are to achieve the desired identification with the people whom they will solicit.

In 1960 Dick Herman thought the foot soldier program might be particularly beneficial in South Omaha—a territory which so far as anyone could remember had never voted Republican.

We anticipated there might be difficulty in enlisting enough volunteers to carry out the project. Registered Democrats outnumbered the Republicans in this area by about three to one.

Herman established his headquarters for the telephone lines in a downtown hotel. He employed professional operators with telephone experience. In the first two weeks Herman's girls called every registered Republican in the target area. The results were encouraging but we were still far short of full recruitment.

The contribution Dick Herman made to this procedure came about after he had exhaused his list of Republicans in the area of solicitation.

"I still need about five hundred workers," Dick told me on the telephone, "and I want to try random calls to the people who live in the neighborhoods where we do not now have a volunteer."

"But they will all be Democrats," I protested.

"I know they will," he told me, "but let's try it for one day. If we get a bad reaction, we'll stop. If the reaction isn't too antagonistic and we pick up some workers, we'll continue."

The results amazed both of us. The number of antagonistic responses was about the same as he had experienced when calling selected Republicans. The number of workers enlisted was about the same.

To confirm the telephone commitment requires prompt action. The volunteer's name and address, with the acceptance verified by the initials of the telephone operator, must move immediately to the mail room. Here a letter of confirmation ending with the personal signature of the candidate is prepared and mailed immediately. The letter should strive to enhance the personal relationship between the cause of the candidate and the volunteer.

"Dear Mrs. Jones: Nina Gleeson has told me that you are going to help us. I am truly grateful and greatly encouraged by your willingness to be an active worker in my campaign.

"The packet of literature Nina told you about will be delivered on such-and-such a date. Mrs. Brunson, who lives not too far from you, will bring it to your house . . . Gratefully yours, Bob."

"Nina Gleeson has told me you are going to help" . . . this is confirmation of a personal commitment on a personal basis. "Mrs Brunson will bring the packet. She lives not too far from you" . . . you are really joining your neighbors in this effort, Mrs. Jones, and don't worry—if you still have some questions, Mrs. Brunson can answer them when she calls.

Now someone is going to make a personal contact, someone who knows that you, Mrs. Jones, told Nina Gleeson that you would work for Bob. Nina told Bob that you said you would work for him. Bob has told Mrs. Brunson that you said you were going to work for him. If you were just trying to be nice to that girl on the telephone and don't really want to help in the campaign, it's too late now, isn't it?

If funds are available, enthusiasm can be further stimulated by including an autographed photograph of the candidate with the letter of confirmation. High quality photographs, complete with signature, can be reproduced by various printing processes quite inexpensively.

On the wall at telephone headquarters there should be a detailed map, one that shows all the streets in the area to be covered. Colored pins on the map will indicate where the volunteers have been solicited. The area should be divided into a comfortable geographical section for the distribution of the packets. A volunteer captain is assigned to each district.

The name of the volunteer solicited is printed or typed on the packet. We have found commercial nine by twelve envelopes suitable for this purpose.

The packet must contain an identification badge or name tag. This strengthens the volunteer's sense of commitment. A printed instruction sheet to inform Mrs. Jones precisely what she is expected to do and enough pamphlets to cover the estimated number of houses in the block are included.

Don't put in a few extra pamphlets. Your volunteers will probably fail to connect with two or three of the householders assigned to their area, and two or three unused pamphlets in each packet can result in a lot of wasted printing.

The instruction sheet is a review of everything we have discussed here. The volunteer is admonished not to engage in any arguments—never to mention the name of the opposition candidate or to speak critically of anyone in the opposition. Then a sample solicitation is outlined:

1. To be used if you know your neighbors on a first-name basis:

"Good morning, Helen, I'm out working for United States Senator Robert Maxwell. He's a good man and I think we need him in the Senate. I hope you and Bill will vote for him. Please read this pamphlet and show it to Bill when he comes home."

2. If the neighbor's name is not known:

"Good morning, I'm Mary Jones. I live at 1012 Elm Street. I'm a volunteer out working for United States Senator Robert Maxwell. He's a good man and I think we need him in the Senate. I'm going to vote for him and I hope you and your husband will, too. Won't you please read this pamphlet? It tells all about Senator Maxwell."

I have explained the neighbors' organization to a dozen different campaign managers. Someone always says: "Why should they vote for a candidate just because their neighbor is voting that way? What kind of a reason is that to choose a United States Senator?"

It is a very good reason indeed—for someone who is not firmly committed to either candidate. If they don't have any strong convictions, the fact that their neighbor has volunteered to solicit votes for Robert Maxwell will provide them with a sort of second-hand personal identification with the candidate himself. If they know the neighbor who is doing the soliciting, their regard and respect for the neighbor becomes an additional reason. If they don't know the neighbor, the fact of their geographical nearness lends strength to the request.

And what about the pamphlet, what does it say? That Senator Maxwell is an expert on atomic energy or has served with distinction on a foreign relations committee or is a member of the Republican Policy Committee? Not by a jugful.

The pamphlet is titled *Neighbors for Maxwell*. The layout is simple. There are pictures of the candidate in a homey atmosphere, pictures of the candidate's wife, pictures of the candidate's children. If the candidate had a humble beginning, it is probable the pictures were taken with the candidate standing on the front porch of his old home. The text emphasizes that neighbors should be for Robert Maxwell because he is a good man who believes in the American family, puts his faith in Almighty God, loves his country and works hard. Corny? Emotional? Yes, indeed.

The great issues of our time absorb the interest of those who are politically sophisticated. Traditional party loyalty will prompt a majority of voters to stay within their own lines. But the undecided voter, the citizen who pays scant attention to the political wars, who is inclined to think that "his vote doesn't count very much anyway," can be motivated to respond to the kind of appeal we are discussing here by an emphasis on those qualities which would make the candidate a good and desirable resident of the neighborhood.

Results which can be readily verified from a foot soldier operation in campaign after campaign argue that when the issues are complex and the competition between candidates is bitter, there is room for simplicity, for neighbor-to-neighbor appeal.

11 | Public Opinion Polls

Public opinion samplings that attempt to predict the winner in an election contest are utterly useless to a candidate and an unnecessary waste of money. Unfortunately, most candidates are suckers for the crystal ball gazers. There is no real way to tell what impact they are making upon the public so they seek solace in the popularity poll.

Practitioners of the polling art have built a great temple of socio-scientific logic. The only poll that counts is the one taken in the voting booth on election day.

The elaborate apparatus that surrounds the scientific counting of the public pulse demands weighted samples, geographical distribution and expert computation of the results. Those of us old enough to remember the Literary Digest poll will have good reason to question the infallibility of Dr. Gallup and his legion of imitators.

The poll takers don't guarantee their predictions will come true. They frequently claim an accuracy of two or three per cent. But there is a sophistry in this claim. If they predict 52 per cent of the vote and candidate Jones only gets 49½ per cent of the vote, the error is described as being 2½ per cent and, from one viewpoint, this is a logical and honest contention. But if the 2½ per cent Jones didn't get is given to Smith, Jones' opponent, the total error comes to five per cent of the voting population and many elections are decided by less than five per cent. Witness the less than 200,000 vote difference in the popular support between candidate Nixon and candidate Kennedy.

The position polls are usually announced by the candidate who is ahead, the theory being that some of the undecided voters will want to join the winner. Numerous imponderables defy prediction. How many citizens will go to the polls? Will bad weather keep a substantial percentage of the people from voting? What about the calculated, last-minute charge of one candidate or the other? Will a national crisis such as the announcement that Russian missiles had been established in Cuba affect the outcome?

Assume the polls are accurate, your candidate is behind and is going to lose the election. Will this permit you to abandon your efforts and concede victory? Of course not.

Newspapers, radio stations and other organizations that derive profit from probing the public mind will, in most cases, sponsor the popularity polls. It is hoped publishing or announcing the results will increase circulation or enlarge an audience. A candidate, his manager and the campaign staff will find more productive ways to spend the money at their disposal.

The position polls, if the sampling is accurate, reflect relative strength and reveal any change that has occurred in the public mind during the weeks of the campaign. So far as the outcome of the election is concerned, it doesn't matter what percentage of popularity your candidate enjoys at the start of the campaign. Such a flat statement must be qualified, of course. If your candidate has no popularity, he shouldn't be in the contest to begin with. The information that will be useful to the campaign management team is to be found in the improvement or deterioration of your candidate's popularity. The candidate who is gaining in public favor always has the possibility of victory. The candidate who is losing public favor will probably be defeated. In any case, both candidates will campaign as vigorously as possible right up to election day. And the advance reports predicting triumph or disaster must be regarded as nothing more than a kind of crystal ball gazing.

The campaign manager with victory on his mind will solicit the public's opinion of his candidate. But the questions asked will be calculated to provide answers helpful to the conduct of the campaign.

In the 1960 presidential contest the pollsters working for candidate Kennedy brought in the information that Kennedy's youthful appearance was a liability. JFK immediately changed the style of his haircut, adopted a more conservative dress and deliberately attempted to appear older and more mature.

The kind of public opinion sampling that enables a candidate to change his attack or alter his strategy or aim at the principal concern of his constituents will pay off on election day.

There are two general areas where, in my experience, public opinion sampling should be an essential part of campaign planning:

Question One has to do with the image of the candidate.

Question Two has to do with identifying the major concerns of the constituency.

Sampling public opinion of the voters to determine the profile of your candidate as he is seen by those who will vote for or against him can be completed during the first few weeks of the campaign.

Professional poll takers interpret the results of their interviews in accordance with a formula based upon the population of the constituency, the occupation, economic status, education, age and residence of the person interviewed. If there are ten times as many brick layers in the constituency as there are doctors, the opinion of one brick layer will count ten times as much as the opinion of one doctor.

The allocation of values in taking a weighted sample requires the service of an expert. In performing their work, most of these professional groups actually sample only a very few opinions and then, by projection, formulate their report. But the divisions of society which do very well to provide a weighted sample for determining, let us say, the public's attitude toward Plymouth automobiles, do not operate with such inexorable force when the question is political. For the purpose of determining the candidate's image, a mass sampling, which can be done quite inexpensively, will produce satisfactory results. I have used the professional poll takers in some cases; I have a great respect for their ability. But a simple questionnaire such as the one illustrated on these pages, widely distributed, will provide an accurate reflection of the public's attitude toward your candidate.

The questionnaire can be printed on inexpensive paper with ample room for the respondent to answer those questions which are not multiple choice. The method for distributing and collecting this sample must guarantee the respondent's anonymity.

The type of questionnaire we are examining is one that I have used in numerous campaigns with only slight alteration to fit a particular candidate. The answer part of the sheet is always folded inside and if locked ballot boxes are provided for deposit of the completed questionnaire, the problem of maintaining anonymity is resolved.

GOOD GOVERNMENT SURVEY

You are being asked to help with this survey because your opinions are vital to good government. As a voter you are a participant in every political decision. Your viewpoint on matters of public interest, on national and local issues, on the selection and performance of a public official, is important.

As a knowledgeable citizen you are being asked to register your judgment, to give your opinion of_____ (name of candidate)_____. Please be frank. Your opinions will be correlated with those expressed by other thoughtful citizens of our state. PLEASE DO NOT PUT YOUR NAME AND ADDRESS ON THIS SHEET.

OCCUPATION

Those who will eventually evaluate these reports do not want to know your name and address. It will be helpful if they can have some information about you.

Employed in trade or business _____
Owner or manager of business _____
Employed in industry _____
Owner or manager of industrial operation _____
Professional _____
Wheat farmer _____
Livestock farmer _____
Farm owner _____
Farm operator _____
Farm worker _____

RESIDENCE

If you live in town or city, please put the population _____
Live on farm _____ Home owner _____ Home renter _____

AGE BRACKET

20–30____30–40____40–50____50–60____
When you have finished filling out this form, will you please deposit the completed form in the locked ballot box?

1. Do your know Senator_____(last name)_____?
    a. Do you know him personally? _____
    b. Have you met him once or twice? _____
    c. Have you seen him but never met him? _____
    d. Have you never seen or met him? _____
    e. Have you never heard of him? _____

2. Would you please write on the following lines either a ten word description or the adjectives which you feel best illustrate Senator_____(last name)_____'s performance as a member of the United States Senate?

_____

_____

3. Which of the following words would you select as most descriptive of Senator_____(last name)_____?
    Friendly _____ Intelligent _____ Considerate _____

Young _____ Vigorous _____ Courageous _____ Skillful
_____ Cautious _____ Determined _____ Experienced
_____ Conservative _____ Liberal _____

---

4. If you were asked to put five words together to describe
Senator (last name)_____ 's outstanding characteristics or abilities, which five would you use?

---

5. Which particular phase of (name)_____ 's service in the
Congress is, to your mind, the most valuable and appealing to
the people of_____(name of state)_____ ?*1

> a. His work in behalf of (name of state)_____ in secur-
> ing projects, etc. _____
> b. The prompt attention he gives to every problem
> presented to him by the people of (name of state)
> c. His work in the Foreign Relations Committee _____
> d. His work on the Senate Labor Rackets Commit-
> tee _____
> e. His constant defense of the freedom of the individual
> and the preservation of those moral standards which
> we have inherited from our religious background.

---

6. Do you believe the people of (name of state)_____ associate
Senator (last name)_____ most closely with:

> Wheat farmers _____ Beef farmers _____ Dairy
> farmers _____ Business groups _____ REA Co-
> operatives _____ School teachers _____?*2

7. Do you believe the people of (name of state) regard (first
and last name) as a:

> Strong advocate of economy _____ As a spender _____
> As a middle-of-the-roader _____ As a conservative
> defender of constitutional rights _____?

---

*1 Name the committee assignments which have earned the Senator
recognition.
*2 These categories illustrate what might be used in a farm state.
Forms should be altered to satisfy the population-occupational demands
of the Senator's state.

8. Do you believe the people of (name of state) would rate (first & last name) as:

> Pro-labor union bosses _____ Anti-labor union bosses _____ One who demands justice for all segments and individuals _____?

9. Do you believe the people of (name of state) would rate Senator _____ as:

> A good representative of the whole state population ___?
> A representative of a special segment of the state population _____?

10. Would you describe the qualities which you believe are (first and last name)   's greatest assets?

_____

_____

11. Would you put down the qualities which you believe are (fiirst & last name   's greatest liabilities?

_____

_____

The questionnaire may be headed *Good Government Survey, Citizenship Opinion,* or *Voters' Viewpoint.*

Please not the first paragraphs:

> You are being asked to help with this survey because your opinions are vital to good government. As a voter you are a participant in every political decision. Your viewpoint on matters of public interest, on national and local issues, on the selection and performance of a public official, is important.
>
> As a knowledgeable citizen you are being asked to register your judgment, to give your opinion of _____ _____ (Insert name of candidate.) Please be frank. Your opinions will be correlated with those expressed by other thoughtful citizens of our state. PLEASE DO NOT PUT YOUR NAME AND ADDRESS ON THIS SHEET.

Now what have we done? We have expressed our admiration for the thinking and opinions of the respondent; we have suggested it is his duty as a citizen to register his opinion. We have guaranteed that he will remain anonymous.

Under the heading *Occupation* we have asked some questions about the man whose opinions we are going to consider, but nothing on this part of the form could lead to identification of the individual. "Those who will eventually evaluate these reports do not want to know your name and address. It will be helpful if they can have some information about you."

Question One with its five subdivisions is designed to permit the campaign manager to discover what percentage of the general public is acquainted with the candidate. It was Section E of this question which produced the shocking information that more than 30 per cent of the people in Nebraska who filled out the questionnaire had never even heard of their present United States Senator Carl Curtis.

Questions Two and Three are probably a little unfair. Question Three suggests words which might be included in the answers to Question Two. But anyone opposed to your candidate will choose his own words. If you can prod the Undecided to associate good words with your candidate, so much the better.

Question Five can prompt some particularly revealing answers. Sub-question C is a plant—the Senator was not a member of the Senate Foreign Relations Committee. Anyone who picked this as his most valuable work was revealed as someone who didn't know much about the Senator.

Questions Ten and Eleven are particularly important. If Ten is answered and Eleven ignored, chances are good the respondent is a stalwart supporter of your candidate. Conversely, if Eleven is answered and Ten is ignored, the questionnaire was probably filled out by a member of the opposition. When both questions are answered and the qualities mentioned can be recognized as being among the assets or liabilities of your candidate, you are probably considering the opinions of a thoughtful, well informed voter.

What the campaign management is striving for with this type

of questionnaire is a mass reflection from a mass audience. There is, however, an additional benefit. If the voters can be prompted to consider the good qualities of your candidate and his past performance, the impression gained will probably be a favorable one.

Similar questionnaires should be prepared and distributed to solicit an evaluation of your candidate's opponent. When the results of these two surveys are placed side by side, the task of finding the major differences, identifying the blacks and the whites, becomes an easy one.

In rural communities it is often possible to enlist the assistance of the editor of a weekly newspaper. Americans like to answer questions, particularly questions about politics. If your questionnaire is fair, if both candidates are treated impartially, widespread circulation can be obtained.

In several campaigns we have had as many as 20 per cent of the voting population respond to this type of questionnaire. A man or woman who is willing to spend five minutes recording his or her opinions of a candidate has moved several steps closer to commitment.

Each respondent is required to give some thought to the questions and more thought to formulating the answers. If the answers are favorable to your candidate, this is beneficial. A voter who has expressed a favorable opinion on the questionnaire will be inclined to vote for your candidate.

The questionnaires may reveal that your man is better known in one area of the constituency than in another. This provides the campaign management with an opportunity to correct the situation well in advance of election day. It may be that your candidate is better known to one class or group of respondents than to another—better known let us say to the farmers than to the city people. And again this information can help the management guide the candidate to victory.

One more benefit from this type of poll deserves to be mentioned. The average American is flattered when asked to give his opinion on any subject. Many people are skeptical of the Gallup poll because they have never met anyone who was interviewed by a Gallup pollster. The mass distribution of the profile questionnaire will enhance any statement your candidate wants to make at a later date. On controversial issues where the electorate is genuinely divided, your candidate can strengthen his position by the argument that the majority of the voters support his position. How does he know this? He has been sampling voter opinion.

The second phase of public opinion sampling concerns the identification of important issues. Experience in a number of campaigns indicates that this single function is perhaps the most important of all aspects of campaign management. If carried out successfully, the results of such a survey will enable your candidate to speak directly to the issues of greatest concern in the minds of the people he is trying to reach.

The purpose of this type of survey is not to find out whether a majority of the people favor one side or the other of an issue. Such a determination would require a very accurate polling apparatus. No candidate can hope to be on the popular side of every issue although many try to do so. And their antics of jumping frantically back and forth invariably convict them of insincerity.

The problem is a simple one. The people in County X are concerned about the Cuban crisis. Some think we should invade Cuba and depose Castro by force. Others think we should avoid war but recognize the danger in the continuation of Castro's government. Your candidate has an understanding of the Cuban situation. The people may not agree with the solution he offers but they will retain a favorable impression; they will listen to what he has to say because of their concern over Cuba.

Let's assume that the major industry in one large area is growing peanuts. In another area the major concern is for a deep water harbor. If your candidate discusses the prospects of a deep water harbor before a peanut-minded audience, they won't be interested or impressed by what he says. If your candidate discusses peanuts before a deep water harbor-minded audience, no one will come away from the meeting with a conviction that your candidate is fit material to hold public office.

Now let's reverse the situation. Your candidate comes to the peanut-minded county, discusses the problems of growing peanuts, exhibits an understanding, and then suggests there is a grave danger in becoming a single economy community, that perhaps the difficulties the peanut growers have been experiencing indicates they might better grow alfalfa or potatoes. His views may be contrary to the popular concept but the fact that he addressed his remarks to the major concern of the community will qualify him in the minds of many voters as a candidate who is on his toes, who has taken the trouble to be informed. And this impression will persist long after the actual content of the speech is forgotten.

Voters do not require that candidates agree with them. They do insist that candidates recognize and appreciate their fears and their problems and indicate some understanding of those problems and fears.

In one of the many campaigns I have helped to manage, the candidate and his staff stubbornly denied there was anything to be gained by what I call the "Issue Questionnaire." The candidate was an ardent golfer and I knew it. After 30 minutes discussing other subjects, I switched the conversation to golf. I happened to have my putter with me. Clubs can be rented at almost any good golf course but a putter is a purely personal weapon. I engaged the candidate in a discussion of the problems of putting. I had him show me his stance, then I deliberately picked it to pieces—he was too erect, his grip was wrong, his stance was awkward—and with each critical suggestion I cited some great golfing authority. Then I dropped a couple of golf balls on the hotel room carpet, suggested the candidate try putting my way. He spent five minutes absolutely absorbed with the problems attendant on trying to knock that golf ball into a glass at the other edge of the carpet. After this exercise we returned to politics and sometime later I deliberately switched the conversation to a discussion of the fine points of quarter horses. The candidate had spent most of his life in a city and while he could recognize a horse as being different from a Mercedes-Benz, this was about the extent of his knowledge. He very promptly lost interest in the conversation and turned to something else. Then I made my point.

"When we were talking about golf," I said, "you were eager to listen. You didn't agree with anything I said but you listened because you were interested. When I started talking about horses, you refused even to carry on the conversation. When you are touring this state, you'd better talk about something in which the voters are interested or they'll give up on you the way you gave up on the horses."

The suggestion that there is a need to seek assistance in determining the major issues in a campaign will invariably be rejected by the old pros. They will argue, and with some measure of authority, that the real issues are those matters under discussion in the public press. This may be valid from a completely national point of view. But elections are won in the precincts and the districts and concerns do vary.

In the 1958 Arizona campaign the nation was suffering from widespread unemployment. The news magazines and even the local press were filled with stories concerning this problem. But with the exception of three localities, unemployment was not an issue in Arizona.

The candidate who wants to be heard by the voter must speak to the issues which concern the voter. To do this he must, in the vernacular, "know what it is that's bugging the voters."

The kind of public opinion sampling necessary to determining the issues must be conducted on a continuing basis. The public passion is constantly changing and in a well organized campaign effort the Cell Group organization is a made-to-order apparatus for this kind of survey.

The procedure is not complicated or expensive and it works. Two copies of the issue questionnaire are sent to each member of the Cell Group with instructions to register his opinions on one and to solicit the opinions of someone who is not a member of his social or economic circle on the second form.

The letter requesting this assistance can strengthen the sense of importance which the manager has given to the Cell Group member. Soliciting the second opinion provides the Cell Group member with a project which makes him an active participant in the campaign.

* The sample used in this chapter is from the 1958 Arizona campaign. We printed the questionnaires two-up on an 8½″ x 14″ sheet of paper. The cost of duplication either by mimeograph or multilith is almost negligible, and the feed-back was extremely valuable.

Over the fifteen months of that campaign effort, in every issue list we sent out we included "more water for Arizona." Arizona is a reclamation state. In a very real sense, the economic well-being of all the residents is dependent upon an adequate supply of stored water.

ARIZONA'S WATER PROBLEMS WERE NEVER SELECTED AS THE PARAMOUNT ISSUE BY THOSE WE POLLED.

Our advertising experts estimated Goldwater's opponent in that campaign spent at least $25,000 on magnificent television spots which identified him as the champion who had helped bring water to Arizona. The segments were beautifully prepared, convincing and informative. That money was wasted. The people of Arizona in 1958 were not concerned about water.

Nebraska is a farm state. Crops under the programs of the agricultural stabilization act provide a major share of the state's income. It would be entirely reasonable to anticipate that the voters in Nebraska would indicate great concern over the various proposals lumped together as the "farm program."

* See page 155.

In 1960 this issue was never number one in the minds of the people in Nebraska. The issue survey clearly indicated the voters of that state were more interested in other problems. The knowledge permitted U.S. Senator Carl Curtis to concentrate on those issues which were the primary concerns of his constituency. There was no need either to attack or defend the many complicated aspects of the federal agricultural legislation.

This type of public opinion sampling is obviously not as accurate as one conducted by personal interview and then computed on the basis of a weighted sample. If the questionnaire had been sent only to members of the Cell Group, the answers might have been distorted. The use of the second questionnaire prevented this. And for the purposes of a campaign, the method described is satisfactory.

The interpretation of a survey can be done by any clerical worker. The issues are rated in order of importance as the respondent views the questions. The ratings are transferred to a master sheet; then it is necessary only to total the figures to determine the number one issue. The lowest total would be Number One, the next Number Two, etc.

After three or four samplings have been made, a consistent pattern will emerge. It is usually possible to find an impressive black and white difference between the position of your candidate and the position of the opposition on these issues which are of greatest concern to the voter.

The importance of candidate identification with the overriding issues can easily be illustrated by a review of the Roosevelt campaign, the Eisenhower campaign and the Kennedy campaign.

The issue of the great depression was given to Roosevelt, but he exploited it. In almost every speech, every statement, every news conference, both as candidate and President, FDR promised action to alleviate the symptoms of the depression—"freedom from fear," "freedom from want." His constant attack on economic royalists, his numerous alphabetical agencies all made

Roosevelt the solid champion of the poor working man and the unemployed.

The war issue in 1940 and again in '44 were handed to Roosevelt but he exploited them beautifully.

In 1952, the Korean War was the over-riding issue. Stevenson's beautiful speeches dealing with an abstract political philosophy lacked the sharp cutting edge of Eisenhower's statement: "I will go to Korea."

The Nixon-Kennedy contest provides a particularly productive subject for study. Senator Kennedy was a regional candidate. He was not a giant in the Senate. Except for those few moments at the '56 convention in Chicago when he was mentioned for Vice President, Kennedy was unknown nationally.

Theodore White's book: "The Making of a President" reveals that following that convention in 1956, Kennedy recruited a staff of able, political technicians and set out to capture the 1960 nomination. The Democrats had four possibilities—Stevenson, Humphrey, Johnson and Kennedy. Humphrey was better known than Kennedy. Johnson had powerful support as the Majority Leader of the Senate and Stevenson was still the darling of Mrs. Eleanor Roosevelt and the controlling wing of the existing Democrat Party.

The Kennedy strategy was geared, first, to "going where the ducks are" and, second, to building an image—youth and vigor —which would place the other aspirants at a great disadvantage.

The Kennedy campaign was almost silent and by its silence gained effectiveness. Kennedy won Wisconsin with organization, money, charm and a better understanding of the concerns of the Wisconsin constituency.

Kennedy's victory in West Virginia was a foregone conclusion. His publicists deliberately built it up into a major contest knowing their candidate would win. And what did Kennedy talk about in West Virginia? The problem of unemployment. He pre-empted the subject. Everything Humphrey said sounded like an echo. The Kennedy team out-smarted all the rest.

In 1960 there was great public concern over the emergence of Castro in Cuba. Kennedy had described Castro in one of his books as a patriot comparable to Simon Bolivar. The liberals had supported Castro's revolution and helped to finance Batista's downfall. Kennedy was extremely vulnerable on the Cuban issue. He turned this into an asset by challenging Nixon; the Republican candidate was forced to make a rather weak defense of the Eisenhower policy.

When Nixon, during the debates, conceded that as a Republican presidential candidate he would endorse all the goals enunciated by Kennedy, he virtually removed the issues and reduced the 1960 election to a personality contest.

The kindest thing which can be said about the Nixon campaign is that it lacked direction. There was no recognizable head. When Nixon met with Rockefeller in New York to discuss the Republican platform, his campaign manager, Len Hall, didn't even know the meeting was scheduled. When the first reports came to Chicago, Hall was furious. It is difficult to say who really managed the Nixon campaign. Bob Finch had some limited authority. Len Hall had to accept public responsibility for the fiasco. But Arthur Flemming and Attorney General Rogers are credited by insiders with Nixon's endorsement of welfare state proposals.

To those of us who were trying desperately to win the election for Nixon, it was painfully apparent that our candidate did not have an overriding strategy and had not selected the issues upon which to build a continuing theme.

When Nixon's advance man came to Arizona he met with 30 or 40 party leaders to arrange for the Vice President's visit. At one point he asked: "What do you think Mr. Nixon should talk about? The Arizona water problem?"

When someone suggested the people of Arizona would be more interested in hearing Nixon's proposals for defeating communism, remedying the Cuban situation and correcting our deficit balance of payments, Nixon's man said: "They care about those things way out here?!"

Nixon did come to Arizona and he made a fighting speech. Many of us who heard it believe that if he had spoken in the same manner before audiences in every section of the country, he would have been an easy winner.

In the '60 election it was so difficult for the voters to find any clear black and white differences between Kennedy and Nixon, they were almost compelled to rest their decision on such unimportant things as the candidate's relatives' appearance on television.

It has been argued that Nixon's illness at the start of the campaign was a liability from which he never quite recovered. The truth is that the lack of a central theme, the campaign's refusal to concentrate on the really important issues, coupled with Nixon's quixotic promise to visit every state, made it impossible to bring the campaign to a peak before election day.

Both private and public polls indicated that Nixon was gaining. Numerous projections indicate that, had the election been held the *third* Tuesday in that November, Nixon would have been the victor.

The Indifferents and the Undecideds who determine the outcome of every election are fickle. The winning candidate must conduct a campaign which will put him *first* in the affections of this group on election day, not 10 days before, not 10 days after.

Sample *ISSUE QUESTIONNAIRE*

You and I as responsible citizens are required to think about the future. We are concerned with the great problems of our day. On this sheet we have listed six of those concerns. Will you help me determine which is most important in your mind and in the minds of your fellow citizens by rating these issues in their order of importance?

Please study the list. Ask the advice of a trusted friend if you like. Then number the list from "1" to "6" giving a

rating of "1" to the issue which you believe to be most important and "6" to the least important. Please try to make
your ratings reflect the thinking of your community.

Gratefully yours,
s/   Bob

☐ Unemployment and the recession.

☐ Federal aid to education.

☐ National defense and the Russian activities in space.

☐ Additional water for Arizona.

☐ The threat of world communism.

☐ The right-to-work law.

12 | Direct Mail

It is generally agreed the most effective solicitation for votes takes place when a candidate grasps the voter's hand with a warm and friendly grip and says "Please vote for me." Because it is impossible today for any candidate to shake the hand of every constituent, political campaigns must utilize every advertising medium known to man.

The only legitimate objective of political advertising is to extend the impact of the candidate's personality and political philosophy. Virtually every candidate for political office uses some kind of direct mailing piece to solicit votes. In the season of politics the average householder will receive from two to twenty pieces of such mail—political circulars, letters, post cards, stickers, buttons and pot-holders. Most of this sizable effort is wasted.

Direct mail is effective only when it can be an extension of the candidate. Unless your mailing piece carries something of the impact of a personal solicitation, it will probably be overlooked between a beautiful and almost irresistible appeal to join the book-of-the-month club and a four-color brochure extolling the virtues of the latest Detroit product.

The businesses of this nation that sell millions of dollars worth of merchandise through the use of direct mail are satisfied when three out of every 100 letters produce a sale. The politicians of my acquaintance naively expect every voter eagerly to read their mailing pieces and unanimously accept and approve the claims made for the candidates.

Newspapers, television and radio are truly mass media. Some slight selectivity can be found as to audience in specialized publications such as the journals that are house organs for the well organized minorities. But for the most part, the political ad on television or radio or in a metropolitan newspaper cannot be aimed at any particular segment of the voting population. Presentation in the mass media calls for the shotgun approach. Direct mail can be aimed like a rifle at a specific target. Because of this selectivity, direct mail in a political campaign can be far more productive. Planning and preparing political direct mail is no job for an amateur. But even the most experienced professional in the field will require a thorough political orientation.

Because of its many commercial uses, the mail order business has become almost a craft apart from all other advertising. The uninitiated will be immediately bewildered by the number of mailing lists available. In most constituencies you can find:

1. Lists of all registered voters.
2. Lists of registered voters segregated as to parties.
3. Lists of registered voters segregated by geographical location of residence.
4. Lists of new voters who have registered in the previous year.

These are the obvious targets for political mail and the only ones most politicians use. The real political gold is to be found in a proper exploitation of the selective lists, such as

1. Lists by income bracket.
2. Lists by occupation:
   Doctors
   Lawyers

Dentists

Independent businessmen

Service station owners

Printers

Farmers

Bankers. . . .

The direct mail expert working on a political campaign should first assemble detailed information on every available mailing list. When this has been done the campaign manager can select the targets, much in the same manner as he determined the area of greatest probable return. What kind of people are most likely to respond to the qualities of your candidate? Where is there a recognizable mutuality of interest existing between your candidate and one of the categories of mailing lists? Is your candidate a prominent farmer? Then by all means the mailing should be sent to farmers. Is your candidate an active churchman? Then the mailing piece should be sent to all of his fellow church members. Does your candidate have a point of view particularly appealing to doctors? Then the doctors' list should be mailed.

We are all familiar with the mechanical typewriters which will mass produce what appears to be a personalized letter, but this type of mailing piece is far too expensive to be used as a general rule. However, effective ways of personalizing the mailing piece can be found once the general profile of the addressee has been determined.

There is a place for the Robo-type or Hooven letter in politics, particularly if your candidate is an incumbent. Members of Congress receive many letters from their constituents. A voter who has demonstrated his interest in politics by writing a letter to his senator or congressman is a likely target for a machine-type letter with personal salutation and signature. Community leaders usually deserve this kind of personalization, but most campaign budgets simply cannot stand the expense required to make large scale mailings of this kind of letter.

How can large scale mailings achieve the effectiveness of personal solicitation? By addressing themselves to the particular interest or situation of the addressee and this can be determined quite accurately by a review of the categories of mailing lists available.

Residents of a generally rural area should be approached with a letter and a special pamphlet addressed to the common concerns of rural residents. In the great cities an entirely different approach will be required and a different pamphlet should be enclosed, one that identifies your candidate with the problems of urban living.

Is your candidate trying to persuade the residents of an industrial district to support his election? Is unionism a problem? If so, a letter that speaks directly to the interests of union members, together with a pamphlet that deals exclusively with your candidate's position on unions, will be read and remembered.

The voters who are registered in the political party of your candidate should receive a letter aimed at exploiting their party interest. But, here again, area of residence will dictate a special letter for party members who live in the country with perhaps an entirely different kind of letter for the party members who live in the city.

No single letter, no single enclosure can be devised that will effectively present your candidate's appeal through every mailbox in the constituency. Newly registered voters, for example, should receive a letter exploiting this situation. The possibilities are infinite.

Members of the campaign staff should be required to list the name of every person in the constituency with whom they have ever had any personal contact. In such correspondence signed by the candidate himself, the relationship should be established in the first paragraph: "Dear Mr. Smith: . . . Bill Jones of Grand Island, who is helping on my campaign, has told me of . . ." Once the entree or bridge is established, the candidate's message becomes compelling and personal.

All direct mail letters should attempt to create a mutual

objective between the writer and the reader. *You* and *we* are the magic words that help to create the feeling of mutual interest.

If the letter is printed or duplicated by any of the usual processes, no attempt should be made to conceal this fact, but this does not mean that it is impossible to create the suggestion of personal communication. In one campaign in which we mailed a letter to every member of our candidate's political party and requested a particular action, the letter began as follows:

Dear Fellow Republican: . . . This is an age of miracles. I am not referring to satellites and guided missiles and such mysterious things as television. This letter is in itself a miracle. It has been reproduced by a camera, printed on an automatic machine—even the address on the envelope was put there by an automatic process. Yet, this is truly a personal message.

You and I are enlisted in the same cause. We serve the same principles of government. We believe in the same future for America. . . .

Every piece of direct mail—pamphlet, letter, post card— must be prepared for a specific target. Each piece should contain an offer of benefit. The need for action must be stressed. And, if possible, it should be a personal appeal for a specific kind of assistance—please give this pamphlet to your neighbor —please put my sticker on the windshield of your car—please watch the television at such a date and time.

Because direct mail can be aimed at a specific target area, it lends itself to utilization in the last two weeks of the campaign. At this point the major concerns will have been identified. Research will have developed the blacks and whites of the differences between your candidate and his opponent and direct mail can exploit these to good advantage.

There must be a logical reason for every mailing. The more pertinent or timely, the greater the reception will be. If your letter can deal with a specific issue which has been raised, reader interest will be heightened. The development of the issues and of the differences between your candidate and his opponent will probably dictate your selection of the most productive mailing list.

Assume for a moment that in the campaign the issue of a method of taxation has been developed. I recall one state campaign where our opponent was strongly opposed to a sales tax and argued instead for an increase of the income tax. Our candidate opposed an increase to the income tax and argued the sales tax as being more equitable. We exploited this natural division by mailing a letter and a pamphlet of our candidate's position to those voters who would suffer most if the income tax were raised.

In every state-wide campaign there are overriding issues and the state-wide candidate in his mass advertising must confine himself to these issues. Not infrequently there will also develop local issues which so far as the voters of that particular locality are concerned become of first importance.

In recent years the planners of federal superhighways have insisted on by-passing small communities. In Arizona and a number of other Western states, communities have developed along the old highway routes which are dependent upon the highway traveler for their economic life. The problem of by-passing is vital to the residents of these communities. Residents of larger cities are frequently eager to have the highways by-pass. Thus, we have a conflict of interest between the voters in a single constituency. In the small highway towns the motels, gasoline stations, garages, restaurants and curio stores are threatened with a serious loss of trade if the proposed new highway carries the traffic around the town.

In 1958 Senator Goldwater was in favor of reasonable by-pass provisions, arguing that existing towns which were dependent upon highway traffic should be protected by planning the new highways to pass within sight of the town and by providing easy access from the highway to the town.

Direct mail addressed to the residents of these small communities was a perfect vehicle for expressing the Senator's views. It was a rifle approach that hit the target in the bull's-eye.

In another chapter we discussed how direct mail was used to distribute the candidate's car stickers, how direct mail assists in the enlistment of the Cell Group. The postcard last-minute appeal is an example of direct mail. The letters and other mailing pieces need not be elaborate, but they must be specific. Don't attempt to disguise a mass-produced letter as a personal communication. Don't begin your letter with "I"; the reader is far more important than the writer. Don't fail to request a specific act of cooperation. Don't standardize on long letters or short letters. Use enough copy to get the message across—and not one extra word. Don't entrust the creation of your direct mail to an amateur.

In one campaign the use of direct mail permitted us to approach that special group we were most eager to reach—the Indifferents. How does someone demonstrate that he or she is not very interested in a political decision? Simply by not voting.

I once had a Republican candidate in a state where registered Democrats outnumbered registered Republicans by a ratio of about three to one. In order for my man to win it was necessary to persuade more than one-third of those voters who were nominally registered in the Democrat Party to cross the line and vote for a Republican. Almost fifty per cent of the population of this state lived in one county, and we were convinced the outcome of the election would be decided by how this county voted.

Immediately following the party primaries I contacted the election officials. The law did not permit anyone to take the great registers away from the courthouse, but these voting records were public property and as such were open for inspection.

Through the cooperation of a county election official I was able to secure permission to have the names copied. We put ten girls to work addressing envelopes. There was no printing on the envelopes and, fortunately for us, no Democrat official got wind of what we were doing. The girls copied the name of every registered Democrat who had failed to vote in the primary. On Friday and Saturday before election Tuesday we mailed a few more than 40,000 letters to these Indifferents. The letters were sponsored by a group of Democrats who were supporting my Republican candidate. The letterhead was non-committal, but the letter was strictly hard-sell, strongly in favor of my candidate, strongly opposed to the Democrat nominee. It bore the typewritten signature of twelve prominent members of the Democrat Party.

By the time the opposition discovered the letter it was too late for them to do anything about it; the polls were closed. The Republican candidate had won, his victory made possible because a great many Democrats crossed the party line. We are confident that the last minute letter convinced a substantial number of nominal Democrats to follow the example of the men who signed that letter and cross the line to vote for a Republican.

13 | Mass Media

Long before the season of politics reaches its climax on election day the public will begin to manifest resentment against the overdose of political advertising. In every election candidates monopolize television screens, overcrowd the radio channels, fill the newspapers with their pleas for votes. In addition to the paid advertising, the public must put up with newscasts and news columns devoted almost exclusively to the great battles for public office. Producing any kind of an advertisement which will claim the public's attention in the midst of all this competition requires great ingenuity. Advertising agencies can be helpful to the campaign manager but the political product is unique . . . totally unlike the soap and the subdivisions, the automobiles and the air travel which claim the attention of advertising men most of the year.

In planning successful political advertisements the qualities and abilities of the candidate must be considered. Any political advertising that fails to deal with those concerns uppermost in the minds of the electorate is wasted effort.

TELEVISION

Television is the most personal of the mass media. Through the magic of television the candidate enters the living room to be seen and to be heard and to be judged.

165

The candidate who can put himself across on TV enjoys a tremendous advantage, but the electronic camera can be cruel as well as kind. Many students of the 1960 election will argue with stubborn persistence that it was Mr. Nixon's failure to match Mr. Kennedy's performance in the great debates which produced defeat for the Republican candidate.

The politician on television must not only outdo his opponent on the same medium; he must also be more appealing and more entertaining and more commanding than the great stars in the world of entertainment, news and sports whose domain he has invaded.

The conventional time segments of television are against the candidate. It may be that an incumbent President of the United States can hold the attention of a TV audience while he delivers a 30-minute speech, but even this is open to question. Certainly the lesser candidates cannot hope to capture any substantial audience for such a lengthy period with a program consisting of nothing more than a camera focused upon a speaker at a rostrum.

The majority of all prime television time is available only in 30-minute segments. Some stations will sell a 15-minute period during the peak audience hour. But these stations are the exception rather than the rule.

The normal reaction to this dilemma is a decision to buy the one minute, 40, 30, and 20-second commercial spots between existing programs. For many candidates this is a wise decision. But the rate structure of television is such that most stations charge almost as much for a spot between two 30-minute segments as they charge for the 30-minute program time.

Daytime television is more flexible. In these off-peak hours the candidate can frequently find 5-minute availabilities. The rates are less because the audience is smaller. But the politician intent on carrying his message to every voter cannot accomplish this objective with daytime TV alone.

In my experience most advertising agencies think in terms of spot adjacencies to highly rated programs and completely overlook the possibility of content. The television audience demands entertainment, amusement and information. Imaginative programs, with exciting content and dramatic presentation, can make a political program on TV just as attractive as a "Bonanza" or a who-dunnit. Political contests possess the same inherent drama that is found in a championship sporting event. Political television which reflects the true dimensions of the contest for public office will claim the audience attention and enlist the loyalty of the viewer in behalf of the candidate.

The advertising agency experts are best equipped to schedule the TV but the campaign team must provide the imagination to employ the time effectively.

Keeping in mind the need for acceleration, it is wise to concentrate at least 50 per cent of the TV budget in the last two weeks before election day. Other candidates will recognize this same necessity. The result may well be an almost steady diet of political programming on the TV channels that serve the major population centers of the constituency.

Ten years ago the number of channels available to any particular viewer were limited. Now, set owners in most communities can choose between a number of stations.

Spot announcements, with good adjacencies, present your candidate to that segment of the audience which is attracted by the adjacent program. The only other way to guarantee audience attention is to arrange a simulcast—that is, have your candidate appear in program time on all of the available television channels. In some areas this is impossible. In all areas it takes careful advance scheduling. In 1958 and again in 1960 a number of the candidates whom I was serving as a consultant were able to buy identical time segments on several TV channels. There is of course some danger of generating animosity on the part of a few viewers who are more devoted to "Gunsmoke" than they are to politics. But the advantages of simulcasting in my opinion outweigh the liabilities.

The political candidate can dominate a TV screen with a live program relayed to other channels by cable or by using identical video tape. The taped program has many advantages. Audiences are accustomed to delayed broadcasts and this offering no longer carries the almost automatic penalty once imposed upon filmed TV programs. Video tape provides an opportunity for editing.

Caution should be exercised. Don't make the video tape too perfect. Your candidate is not an actor or an entertainer and sometimes the slip or the fluff should be deliberately used to strengthen the sense of audience participation.

All political advertising must be planned to emphasize the image of the candidate and stress the overriding issues. Successful political television makes the greatest demand upon the ability of the campaign manager. Too often the political candidate approaches TV as though it were radio with a picture. *The television camera must be used to carry a visual representation of the message in support of the audio portion. It is this dual impact which gives TV its great persuasive power.*

How is this to be done in a political campaign?

Deliberately and consciously direct the television producers to create a presentation which would carry the story if the audio portion were eliminated. Then use audio as though it were the only aspect of TV.

Numerous examples will occur to anyone who considers the desirability of such planning. In the past I have taken candidates into an open pit mine, into a wheat field, surrounded them with props and supported them with experts.

National defense is always a problem. If your candidate is knowledgeable on matters of defense, don't let him stand up in front of the studio camera. Take the camera to a location—to a military installation, a defense project, a missile silo. Let your candidate stand on the wing of a military aircraft if he is qualified to be there. And when he speaks of national defense against this background, he won't have to tell the audience that he knows what he is talking about.

In one campaign where the farm issue was paramount, we took a camera crew into the field where the tractors and combines were working. The audio of that five-minute segment was devoted to a discussion between the candidate and the farmer. The background noise from the farm machinery made it difficult to hear what either man was saying. But no viewer could question the authenticity of the candidate's interest in and knowledge of farm problems.

One candidate who happened to be a reserve general in the Air Force and a qualified jet pilot, was used in a five-minute segment which showed him climbing out of an aircraft. Against this background, wearing his flying suit, holding his helmet as a prop, the candidate discussed the necessities of adequate air defense.

This use of background can be equally convincing in the spot time segments. If water conservation or reclamation or the development of adequate recreational facilities has a bearing in your campaign, put your candidate in a background where the camera can tell at least one half of the story.

The longer TV program segments require more imagination, and more production. But here again the camera can, in many instances, tell the story more forcefully than the candidate.

In 1958 I was managing a candidate for the Senate who was accused of being anti-union. The union newspapers wouldn't accept his advertisements. The unions wouldn't permit him to appear at their meetings. So we used television.

We made an 8′ x 12′ enlargement of a union newspaper carrying a derogatory headline about the candidate. We set this up as a screen. When the program opened, the candidate was behind the newspaper. We could hear his voice but we could not see him. He told his audience that he had been trying to get through the union's "Paper Screen" to talk directly with the men and women who worked with their hands and the tools. Then he broke the paper barrier and came through the screen— a most dramatic and effective opening.

On that program we used a number of visual aids—cards, charts, props. The day following this presentation more than 100 union members stopped at our headquarters to tell us that after seeing the program, they understood the candidate's position and would vote for him.

Careful consideration should be given to the background for the program segment on TV. Politicians prosper when they are before an audience. The crowd noise and applause add to the drama of the show. Time should be allowed for the camera to pan the audience, to pick up planned reactions, to mirror the empathy between the candidate and the voters.

The audience should be carefully selected to include citizens from every corner of the constituency. If the viewer in Miller- ville sees some familiar faces in the audience, there is a subtle transfer of reality and the voter is influenced favorably.

Don't let your candidate talk for 25 minutes. Use film clips from newsreels or segments made in various sections of the state to illustrate the issue your candidate is discussing. If we employ the peanuts and the deep water harbor similes once more, let your candidate comment on film clips of how peanuts should be grown and processed, or maps and charts of where the deep water harbor should be built.

All voters hope to find a candidate who is knowledgeable, who demonstrates an acquaintance with their problem. They don't demand genius, they don't insist that their candidate know everything about everything and they are really not interested in hearing the candidate dwell on his own virtues.

Successful political programs can be created for any political candidate. With time, money and imagination the camera can qualify your candidate as a man who is competent to meet the needs of his constituency. An adequate TV production will present your hero in such a way as to enhance his stature and at the same time present your candidate in direct contrast to the opposition. If the script is adequate, it will magnify your candidate's assets and at the same time reflect the opposition's liabilities.

I once knew a successful candidate who could not make a speech, who had a shy and retiring personality, who had no particular training for the technical position he sought. But this man was the world's champion horseshoe pitcher. This was long before television, but this man pitched horseshoes in front of every voter who would stand still long enough to watch him. The people elected him and re-elected him and re-elected him because they were impressed by his superior ability. The fact that they were not hiring him to pitch horseshoes on the public payroll made little difference.

Good television spots require the same imaginative approach demanded by the 30-minute segments. Usually it is more difficult to make a real impact in 20 or 30 seconds. But the professionals in this field can take any single idea and sell it within the limitations of the spot time segment.

In a 30-minute period the candidate's appearance and personality and words can enlist the support of the viewers without any real hard-sell vote-for-me approach. The spots require a different treatment. *Ask* the viewer to vote for your candidate and *name him*. Tell the viewer to vote for your candidate and *name him*. Imply that everyone else is going to vote for your candidate and *name him*. Then show or tell the reasons. But keep your candidate in character. If he is a homely man, let the camera record that fact. If he is an intellectual, keep the pitch in that vein. If he is an activist, show him in an active situation. Don't remake the candidate to conform with someone's concept of what a successful television image might require.

The hard-sell spots are usually more effective if the plea and the instruction is given by someone other than the candidate. But show your candidate's picture; show his name; show him in the background that will qualify him as an expert.

To date we have discussed only those television appearances which are sponsored and paid for by the campaign committee. Any candidate for a major office will find numerous opportunities to appear on interview-type shows and other sustaining or commercially sponsored station productions. These appearances must be carefully planned. On interview shows or televised press conferences the candidate must be prepared. Here the manager functions as tormentor and devil's advocate. The full talents of the staff should be utilized to formulate the kind of embarrassing questions which can be expected from newspapermen in the usual no-holds-barred-we'll-get-the-truth-for-you forum show.

If the candidate enters this arena adequately prepared, he can make his greatest gains when responding to unfair questions. Tolerance, not temper, is the key note. The candidate must respond to his tormentors by mentioning their names. If he has spoken on a subject, refer to the full text of this discussion. If the question is a truly sticky one, advise your candidate to quote one or two authorities on the subject. And above all, remind your candidate that he must be in command of the presentation. Some questions deserve a "yes" or "no" answer. In some instances a truthful "I don't know" is much better than an obvious equivocation. What the audience needs is assistance in recognizing your candidate as a product quite different from his opponent. And the short, authoritative friendly response helps to define those differences.

Candidate coffees have become extremely popular and very effective. They are arranged in homes by supporters and permit the candidate a chance to speak and to shake hands with 40 or 50 voters. Obviously, a man running in a large constituency can't find the time to attend enough coffees to make much of an impact. But the TV coffee can extend the area of influence.

Morning television time is relatively inexpensive. The coffee can be arranged with 30 or 40 people in the studio asking questions. The candidate should answer the questions without any reference to notes and should try for a completely informal, off-the-cuff presentation.

A candidate who is gifted on television can do a coffee all by himself. The format of the program is to have someone at a telephone receiving questions from the viewers. Of course it will be necessary to have some of the questions prepared in advance, but these can be solicited in advance and the name of the questioner should be read on the air. The candidate has a cup of coffee but no time to drink it. The atmosphere to create is that of the candidate being in the home of the viewer at a private coffee session.

This type of program has been used in two campaigns of my experience with great effect. By identifying the person who supplied the question, the program becomes an exchange between the candidate and the voter. And by selecting the proper questions, the candidate can address himself to those major issues which have been previously identified by his research group.

Informal, inexpensive and extremely effective—such presentations can be expected to create comment and attract considerable audience.

RADIO

In the great frenzy to embrace the new medium of television, there was a period when radio was almost totally neglected. This is no longer true. The experts who buy time on radio and TV and space in the newspapers to move merchandise have rediscovered the truth: there is always somebody, somewhere, listening to radio.

There are more radio sets in automobiles than there are television sets in homes. The household with one TV set usually has three or four radios. Radio is companionable. It doesn't demand your full attention in the same way television claims its audience. Radio is far more flexible than present day television.

Here again the campaign manager must employ the services of an expert. The notion that anyone can write selling radio copy has long since been proven a fallacy. Radio can be compelling, dramatic, informative. The medium of persuasion is the voice or the sound which must cloak the words with attention-getting conviction. Because radio is more mature than its younger sister, television, the art in this field has reached a higher stage of development. And the cost of radio is extremely modest when compared to the prices charged for TV time.

Someone will say that nobody listens to a 15-minute speech on radio. The audience will hang on your words for 30 minutes if the content deserves their attention.

In those early days when I was managing my first political campaigns, radio was our only electronic medium. We always presented the candidate on radio as the campaign came to a climax, but we never let him sit down in a studio and read a speech. We created a function, clothed it with the trappings of a special event, used a well known radio voice to describe the color of the ceremonies or proceedings, never introduced the candidate until the program had been in progress for at least two or three minutes. That required clearance, "This is a paid political broadcast," loses some of its effect when the candidate has a two or three minute separation from the disclaimer. Any performer does better when supported by an audience. The applause adds to the credibility for those who hear the proceedings. In one minute on radio a competent announcer can make a very effective pitch for a political candidate.

One effective method of impressing a radio audience is to irritate. In one campaign where we had very little money we used two voices, two housewives gossiping over the back fence, talking about the candidate. The script was written purposely with incomplete sentences. One of the gals with a deep Irish brogue emphasized all the candidate's strong points or assets. The other participant in this dialogue quietly and without rancor compared the good things about our candidate with the inadequacies of the opposition. Four and one-half minutes of two women talking over the back fence. In three days we exposed this so many times it would have been impossible for anyone who owned a radio set not to have heard the dialogue at least twice.

By various devices well known to the radio profession, we constantly sampled the audience reaction. When the irritating repetition had produced a real impact, we pulled all the recordings off the air. We had hoped to do this on Monday before election Tuesday but the effect actually peaked on Friday befor the election Tuesday. I felt sure that if we continued the broadcasts, some of the voters would vote against my candidate to express their irritation. It may be that some of them did anyway, but we won that contest and our sampling the day after election revealed that more voters had heard the radio dialogue or, at least, remembered hearing it than were affected by any other single advertisement on any of the media.

When planning a radio program, remember to insert some distinctive identifying format—sound, voice, something—which will instantly inform the listener he is hearing about *your* candidate. In one campaign we used a whistle; another, a trumpet; in a third the roll of a drum; and once I used the Sheriff's siren.

NEWSPAPERS

Political advertising in newspapers can be divided into four general categories . . . message ads, reminder ads, testimonial ads and black-type ads.

The message advertisement in a newspaper carries a short positive statement from your candidate. In order to heighten the public understanding of the conflict, this type of appeal should carry a positive and a negative. Your candidate believes certain things; the opposition does not believe these things. Your candidate is committed to a particular course of action; the opposition is opposed to this course of action. Or, the opposition is committed to a course of action; your candidate is opposed to this course of action.

Message ads will have greater impact if they carry identification, a format distinctively different permits the reader to make instant recognition.

Reminder ads are usually smaller in size, oftentimes not more than two columns by two inches, and usually carry nothing more than the picture, distinctive identification, and either a plea for votes or an instruction to vote for the candidate. Some readers respond better to a command which says "Vote for Congressman Jones" than they do to a request stating "Please vote for Congressman Jones."

In my experience the candidate can maintain his impact in the newspaper by alternating between the message-type ad and the reminder-type ad, but the layout or pattern must promote instant recognition.

Many candidates favor the testimonial-type ad. These are usually one column by six or eight inches. They feature the picture of a prominent citizen and carry his statement as to why he or she will vote for the candidate. Minority and special interest groups are frequently persuaded to follow their group leaders to the polling place.

The fourth type ad which I call "black type" is probably more familiar as "the political ad." It carries considerable copy, the type is large and it literally screams the virtues of the candidate or the vices of the opposition. A black type ad is indicated whenever your research has developed a serious defect in the opposition.

In one campaign our research department came up with the information that the opponent, speaking before a community group, had made a flat statement which was offensive to all PTA members. This was material for a black type ad. Another time, an opponent had a police record which he had carefully concealed from the voters. This prompted a black type ad. Facts can be stated bluntly. But where your opponent in the past has been guilty of bad or unwise association, understate the issue.

In one campaign we had incontrovertible evidence that the opponent had at one time been a member of the Communist

Party. A number of people on our campaign staff wanted to do a black type ad and make the charge that our opponent had been a communist.

The nation had just gone through the McCarthy hearings and the liberal press was ready to do battle for anyone accused of being "pink." I decided we could get more mileage out of the information by understating our case. We did a black type ad, but the copy merely suggested that our opponent had at one time been associated with the Communist Party.

The liberal press reacted beautifully. We were accused of attempting to establish guilt by association and almost every newspaper in the state carried the story of our charge and the defense which was offered against it.

In our second blast we said "yes, we had suggested that the opponent might be a communist, but we weren't practicing guilt by association" and we printed proof of the charge.

In almost every political contest understatement of facts which you believe to be real blockbusters will open the door for offering the proof of the implied charge to an eager, and usually skeptical, audience.

Every manager of a political campaign must learn to differentiate between the legitimate advertising media and what I call "the blackmail papers." In the season of politics, numerous publications appear. They are sponsored by lodges, by associations, by minority interests. They all demand a share of your advertising.

Almost invariably the candidate will suggest propitiating these people by inserting some small ads in every paper. In a number of campaigns I have instructed our agency to deny advertising placement to any publication of this type. My refusal has brought some rather warm and colorful language my way, but it never cost a candidate an election.

Legitimate news publications with verified circulation and a history of regular publication should rightfully receive that portion of the candidate's newspaper advertising budget which corresponds to the circulation guaranteed.

Weekly newspapers, even in areas served by metropolitan dailies, should be given special consideration. The weekly newspaper is usually read because of hometown or community loyalty. The big daily is busy exposing the evils of society and saying unkind things about people. The weekly is filled with hometown gossip and complimentary comments. The readers of the weeklies invariably have greater affection for the editorial opinion and the editorial content of these smaller newspapers than is held by the subscribers to the metropolitan daily press.

Dividing the political budget between television, radio, newspaper, billboard, direct mail and pamphlet printing is an individual problem which does not respond to generalization. Advertising agencies can usually be extremely helpful with advice on the allocation of budgets, but this warning is worth repeating: Political candidates are not like shoes or soap and the advertising budget should be divided after deciding where your candidate is a star. Is he excellent on television? Then this medium should receive major emphasis. Is he better when the voters hear him but do not see him? Use radio. If your candidate has difficulty selling himself on radio and TV, then pour your money into the newspapers. The manager's major responsibility in this area is to be sure that the advertising budget buys enough of the voters' attention to warrant the cost.

PAMPHLETS, CARDS AND POSTERS

Millions of political pamphlets are printed every year. Some of them are very effective. Every candidate wants a brochure. The mistake here is that too many candidates are content with a single printed piece.

If your candidate is a one-dimensional personality, with a one-track mind, with a single asset, then you can do him justice with a single printed piece. But if your candidate combines a number of competencies, if he is knowledgeable in a number of fields, if there are many sides to his personality, then you need a separate pamphlet to reflect each major asset.

I was once called into a gubernatorial campaign very late in the political season. I discovered there had been no printing done for the candidate, but I was assured by his managers that the copy was almost ready and we would have "the brochure" in a couple of weeks. Finally, by being obnoxiously insistent, I secured the copy which had been prepared. It was beautiful. Nine thousand words. Anyone reading the copy would have been convinced that our candidate had somehow combined in one person all the virtues of Washington, Jefferson, Lincoln, Wilson and Daniel Boone. I had a little trouble with Daniel Boone. I didn't see why the fact that our man had been born in Kentucky made him necessarily the voters' choice to be governor of a Western state.

I cut the copy as much as I could and the campaign staff finally accomplished the printing. Then they ran a full-page ad duplicating the pamphlet. (About $1800 worth of newspaper space filled with 10-point type.) When the candidate showed it to me, my comment was: "Your mother may read it, but no one else will."

There is a drab, stereo-typed, repulsive similarity to most political pamphlets. The candidate was born. This is an accomplishment he has in common with every other breathing human being. Sometimes there is a glowing description of the candidate's mother and father. This is usually followed by a lengthy recital of accomplishments and the piece ends with a photograph of the candidate's family group.

Effective political campaign pieces translate the assets of the candidate into a desirable qualification which will permit the candidate, if elected, to satisfy a major desire of the constituency. If your candidate has been a successful businessman and one of the issues is governmental fiscal policy, by all means relate this business experience as proof that your man has the competence to discharge the fiscal responsibility he is seeking.

If your candidate is a lawyer and has written desirable legislation, translate this into a promise of future beneficial legislation. What your candidate has done for the voters, if substantial, will argue what he will do in the future. The pamphlet will be particularly effective if it demonstrates the measurable differences between your candidate and the opposition. A pamphlet which outlines your candidate's views on unions and unionism will not interest the rural population. A pamphlet which demonstrates your candidate's competency to deal with problems of the farmer will not make any votes in the big city.

The list of available advertising specialties designed for sale to political candidates has no end—jewelry, buttons, pot holders, balloons, matches. At best, such items can only serve a single function: to make the candidate's name familiar. But what is printed on the matchbook you have in your pocket right now? If you even noticed the printing, you are unusual. If you can remember what it says, you are remarkable. This does not mean that printed book matches are a total waste of money. The policy to adopt with specialties is caution. If the specialty will serve a specific purpose, use it. Don't be seduced into believing that cost should be the deciding factor.

BILLBOARDS AND OUTDOOR ADVERTISING

In the seasons of politics, thousands of eager candidates smile invitingly at the passing parade from the surface of billboards. I have yet to encounter a candidate who has been able to win a contested office without using outdoor advertising.

In 1959 and 1960 when I was attempting to advise active managers of so many campaigns for the United States Senate, my first suggestion was—buy your billboard space now. This advice was offered in May of 1959. It took some additional urging, but by December of 1959 the billboard space for most of these candidates had been bought and paid for.

What's the hurry? There are only so many choice billboard locations in every constituency. When the season of politics rolls around, most of the outdoor advertising companies try to allocate 100 per cent or 200 per cent showings to each party. But, with few exceptions, they simply don't have the available space to give a candidate 100 per cent or 200 per cent showing.*

In the Massachusetts campaign of 1960, Chuck Colson contracted for the Saltonstall boards 10 months in advance of the scheduled showing. When the campaign was over, he told me that Saltonstall's opponent, Thomas J. O'Connor, didn't have a single billboard in Massachusetts—there weren't any available.

Political billboards are normally displayed about 60 days. If the campaign fund is particularly flush, the posting might be extended to 90 days.

The normal two-month period has one inherent drawback. After 30 days the message, having been seen once or twice, no longer attracts attention. The symmetry of the design, the location of the picture, the colors, no longer challenge the eye.

If your billboard poster is to be up more than 30 days, plan to change it in some significant manner at the end of the first month. The billboard posting is done on a 30-day schedule and you can have additional paper pasted in place for a very nominal charge.

I have learned that a competent designer can plan in advance for a change—for an addition of a splash of color or a change in wording—and this can be effected by pasting a small streamer over the original sign.

In one campaign for an incumbent United States Senator we added a red streamer with white letters carrying the words "Re-elect." The streamer was pasted across one corner of the original billboard paper. It changed the geometry, it changed the color effect, it changed the wording. It made a brand new poster and the additional printing for all of the billboards we bought that season cost less than $25.00.

---

* *100 per cent showing—sufficient boards to assure that everyone in a given area will have seen the message at least one time.*

200 per cent showing—sufficient boards to assure that everyone in a given area will have seen the message two or more times.

In one campaign the artist designed a spot to be superimposed, a square of bright orange paper changed the design and the impact of the poster.

In some states the use of small placards is discouraged. But every candidate must have something of this sort, if only to satisfy the demands of friends and supporters. The outdoor billboards, posters, small display cards should all carry a distinctive identifying pattern—something to promote instant recognition. Transit cards for display either inside or outside a public vehicle should carry the poster theme of the campaign.

The Burma Shave jingle signs have produced extremely good results in a number of my campaigns. Variations of this type of display will suggest themselves. Somewhere in every campaign there is room for a light touch.

Bucky O'Neill charged up San Juan Hill with Teddy Roosevelt and died a hero's death. There is a great equestrian statue in the courthouse square of Yavapai County, Arizona. But Bucky is remembered not as a hero but as the most delightful candidate who ever campaigned for the office of sheriff back in the days when Arizona was still a territory.

Cowboy, miner, writer, newspaper editor—Bucky brought a sense of humor to his efforts to win political office. His first announcement bluntly admitted there were probably other men better qualified to serve in that post than Bucky O'Neill, but he wanted the job and needed it.

All of the other candidates were deadly serious. Bucky conducted a whimsical race. Who was elected? Bucky O'Neill, because he made it easy for the voters to recognize the difference between his candidacy and that of his opponents. This is the ultimate goal of all political advertising. The voters who will tip the scales for victory must find the difference before they make the decision.

14 | Don't Let Them Steal It from You

"We was robbed" is a familiar cry. When applied to the outcome of an athletic contest or a business deal, the protest is often recognized as an alibi. The sordid history of vote fraud and stolen elections, which is a part of the American political record, has made politics a dirty word. This being an imperfect world, populated by imperfect men, it would be naive to expect that man's sinful greed which prompts him to steal, lie, cheat and wage war would be submerged or held in check when the contest is for a political prize.

Every political campaign is an intensely partisan effort. Candidates, managers and contributors combine to win a personal victory for the candidate and the party. The prevention of election fraud is a public service. The democratic process by which we attempt to govern ourselves is seriously threatened when the integrity of the ballot can be questioned.

All politicians piously proclaim their devotion to public service. The best evidence of that devotion can be found when candidates and managers support a vigorous enforcement of the election law. The police and the courts need the help of effective political organization to achieve this objective. Enforcement agencies do not have the manpower or the training adequately to supervise the polling places on Election Day. This work must be performed by conscientious volunteers who have been given adequate training for the task.

Once a fraudulent vote has been cast and counted, it is difficult if not impossible to correct the error. The secrecy of the ballot in this country gives the dishonest as well as the honest vote equal standing once the tally has been made. It is relatively simple to prevent an unqualified voter from voting. It is almost impossible to change the outcome or even to detect the fraud after the ballot has been placed in the box or the voter has been permitted to use the machine.

All elections are supervised by officials of political subdivisions of the states. State law establishes the qualifications for voting, designates the polling places and provides the necessary personnel. Paper ballots, which were once universally employed, are gradually being replaced by voting machines.

To insure an honest vote and an honest count, observers, supported by all contending factions, should police the activities in the polling place from the moment the doors open until the last ballot is counted. Every qualified person must be permitted to cast his or her ballot. Every unqualified person must be prevented from casting a ballot.

Most states require the voters to be registered in the precinct of their residence several months prior to election day. Some states permit a citizen to vote after making an affidavit of residence which certifies that the individual is a bonafide resident of the precinct, has been a resident for the required length of time and is therefore entitled to vote. Anyone who files a false affidavit is subject to severe penalty.

This promised punishment does not always protect the ballot. In one city in North Dakota in 1960, more than 500 people voted on affidavits of residence. Following the election, these people could not be found at the residence given. In many cases the street address on the affidavit proved to be fictitious. Great emphasis is placed upon making the privilege of the franchise available to every qualified citizen. The North Dakota law makes it easy to vote but virtually impossible to protect the integrity of the outcome.

Elections are properly policed by poll watchers and challengers. These volunteer citizens, if they are to accomplish their assignment, must be given adequate advance preparation.

In many areas the official charged with conducting the election operates a training session to instruct the officials employed at the polls—judges, inspectors, clerks, etc. Poll watchers, recruited on a volunteer basis, should be instructed to attend these training sessions wherever possible. But, at best, such instruction is usually perfunctory.

The campaign manager or the party chairman should enlist the volunteer poll watchers well in advance of election day. These individuals should be assembled in convenient public meeting places and given a thorough instruction. The applicable election law should be explained, the valid reasons for challenging must be covered and the poll watcher should become part of a carefully organized election day procedure.

It is vital to prevent fraudulent votes being cast. It is equally essential to the process of democracy to bring all eligible voters to the polls. These two objectives must not be confused.

Challengers are in attendance on election day to prevent fraudulent voting. Poll watchers are frequently used to enable the party to bring out the votes.

The poll watching process has been described in many publications. It is relatively simple and will operate effectively wherever the party or the candidate has sufficient volunteer manpower.

The poll watcher is given a copy of the great register for his precinct. As the citizens come in to vote, he checks off their names. By eleven or twelve o'clock on election day the party machinery should begin a concentrated effort to get qualified residents who have not voted to come out during the afternoon hours.

In my experience a card system has been useful. As a citizen votes, his card is placed in the "voted box" by the poll watcher. At eleven o'clock the "voted box" is sent to the party's precinct headquarters. By a process of elimination workers in the precinct can determine those who have not voted and either by telephone or personal calls, the work of getting slow voters to the polls commences.

The AFL-CIO COPE organization, which has been very effective in many elections, has done an excellent documentary on this subject called *The Wisconsin Story*. This begins with volunteers determining who are the friendly voters in a precinct. Then on election day these same volunteers make it their business to take all of the friendly voters to the polls.

The duties of poll watcher and challenger cannot be combined. Unfortunately, this has been attempted in many elections with the result that neither function is adequately served. The challenge operation begins with the precinct records which were compiled by the research department early in the campaign. These must be brought up to date after the registration lists are closed. Challengers must be provided with an accurate list of every citizen who is qualified by registration to vote in the precincts under watch. If this number has fluctuated widely in the past several elections, an attempt should be made to spot check the neighborhood. The fraudulent vote usually begins with a fraudulent registration.

Election officials are required by law to give a ballot to every individual whose name appears on the registration list. They have no way of determining whether or not the registration is valid. This is the job for the volunteer challenger.

Following the 1960 presidential election, evidence was developed to indicate that a number of unqualified voters were permitted to vote in certain precincts in Chicago. Some 30-odd votes were cast by people who claimed to reside in a building which had been demolished prior to election day.

There is a simple, effective and relatively inexpensive way

to check the validity of the registration lists. About two weeks before election a first class letter should be mailed to every registered voter in a suspected precinct. The face of the envelope should bear the instruction: "Please do not forward," and a return address must be printed on the envelope.

The mailing need not be identified as coming from a political organization. If the campaign manager believes the opposition will attempt to cast some fraudulent votes in a particular precinct, he will probably want to adopt some harmless and innocent identity. The letter ostensibly could be authored by a civic betterment society or a charitable organization.

If the addressee is not available to receive mail at the address on the outside of the envelope, the cover will be returned to the sender. The courts have held that when the post office is unable to deliver first class mail to an individual at a specific address, this can be accepted as evidence that the individual does not in fact reside at that address.

The returned undeliverable letters should be given to the challengers. If any individual whose letter has been returned attempts to vote, that individual should be challenged on the ground that he or she is not a bonafide resident of the precinct.

The challengers will frequently encounter hostility. The challenged voter will protest and in some cases the election officials will protest. If there is a genuine conspiracy to encourage the casting of fraudulent ballots, the election officials may attempt to permit the questioned voter to cast a ballot despite the protest.

To protect your challenger, particularly in those precincts where your party is in the minority, it is essential to provide support. Long before election day the manager should enlist a special task force. Young lawyers are particularly suited to this job. But the supply of young lawyers is usually limited and it will be necessary to augment the force with intelligent, determined citizen volunteers.

The task force should be carefully schooled in the election

laws of the constituency. Each member should be equipped with a digest of the pertinent sections of the law and should also have a full copy of the state election laws.

In a large city it is desirable to establish several neighborhood headquarters so this special task force will be available during the hours the polls are open. When the challenger encounters difficulty, he can send for reinforcements.

In one city of 500,000 population we had more than 300 trained workers prepared to answer calls for assistance on election day. The first call for help came about 20 minutes after the polls opened. We sent eight men, four lawyers and four prominent businessmen, to the polling place where the challenger had questioned a voter on the basis of a returned first class letter.

The men on this flying squad recited the law to the election officials. They secured an admission from the challenged voter that he had recently moved from the precinct but had come back to vote, thinking it would be all right. The leader of the task force promised he would make it his personal obligation to see to it that the election officials spent that night in jail if they permitted any violation of the election law.

Our particularly worrisome precincts in that election consisted of voters who were predominantly registered in the opposite party. We received a number of calls for help between six o'clock in the morning and nine-thirty a.m. Then the calls tapered off. The word had been spread through the neighborhood that if you were not qualified to vote, you better not try it. In that election some 5000 fewer ballots were cast in these precincts than had been cast just two years earlier.

Most polling places maintain accurate and duplicate records of the number of qualified voters who have been given a ballot or admitted to the voting machines. The poll watcher should keep an independent tally. In a suspected precinct this effort should be carried on openly in order to inform the election officials of the fact that their records will be checked at the end of the day. Such an obvious check-off will discourage any attempt to stuff the ballot box.

In machine precincts the poll watcher should insist upon witnessing an inspection of the machine tallies before the polls open. Voting machines are usually delivered to the polling place sealed and certified by the Commissioner of Elections. Sometimes voting machines are subject to mysterious failures. They may arrive with a substantial total for one candidate on the machine at the time it is installed. In one election our challenger discovered that two of the four machines being used failed to register a vote for the Republican candidate for governor. These machines were disqualified until a mechanic corrected the malfunction.

When voting machines are used, the matter of verifying the total is usually a simple procedure. The challenger, who is permitted by law to witness the tally when the polls are closed, should keep his own record of the totals on each machine. Most election officials are honest but sometimes numbers are transposed on reports. In those precincts where past action warrants suspicion, an attempt should be made to have the machines impounded under supervision immediately after the polls are closed.

Paper ballot precincts ordinarily produce more error than machine precincts. The tedious task of counting the paper ballot votes sometimes occupies the election board until sunup the day after election. Human beings, weary from a day's service on an election board, frequently make honest mistakes. It is in these long, drawn-out periods of counting that dishonest election officials find an opportunity to influence the outcome of the election.

Most states authorize the political parties to send official watchers to check the count. These watchers must be trained by someone familiar with local practice. In a hotly contested race it is wise to give the official checker an automatic counter. When the tally clerk calls out a vote for a candidate, the watcher can automatically record this.

If there is more than one hotly contested race, additional checkers should be sent to observe the counting. In addition to the number of ballots marked for your candidate vis-a-vis the number marked for his opponent, an attempt should be made to keep track of the total number of ballots. Remember that not all voters mark their ballots for every candidate. Little automatic tally devices, such as those used by door keepers to count attendance, can be very helpful. Your watcher, with both hands in his pockets, can score the opponent's votes with his left hand while counting your candidate's votes with his right.

Most election officials are scrupulously honest. Be wary of those who want to postpone the counting, who suggest that time be taken out for dinner or for coffee breaks. If this occurs, stay with the ballots even though they may ostensibly be locked away in a safe place.

When all the results are in it is wise to review the figures. If the normal turnout has been 80 per cent, you should be suspicious of the precinct which votes 95 per cent.

Poll watchers can frequently detect other improper actions on election day. If the voter comes into the polls bearing an instruction card, it is time to call for help. In most states the law prohibits the bringing of any political literature inside the polling place.

In the 1960 West Virginia primaries hundreds of voters were observed bringing to the polls a card bearing the slate of recommended candidates put out by one of the political organizations. These voters were not challenged but they should have been.

If your election day task force includes volunteers assigned to help get out the vote, it will pay to keep a constant check on the percentage voting in every precinct. If the vote is running extremely heavy in certain areas, you can accept this as an indication that someone is working those precincts skillfully and persistently.

Volunteer challengers sometimes get the notion they are not really contributing a great deal when they spend hour after hour in the polling place on election day without having to make a single challenge. It *is* a tedious assignment but the presence of challengers has a salutary effect upon those who may be planning any illegal action.

Many elections have been won or lost by just one vote in each precinct. Remind your volunteers of this. If their day of duty results in preventing just one illegal ballot, they may have made a major contribution to the integrity of that election. The days and weeks of the campaign effort, the labor of thousands of volunteers, plus all the money you spend, hangs in the balance on election day. If the polls are not policed, the victory you have earned may be stolen.

The day the campaign starts is the time to start planning your security measures for election day. Then, when all the ballots are counted, win or lose, you and all those who have worked with you will find satisfaction in the knowledge that you did everything you could do to advance your candidate, your philosophy, and to contribute to the effectiveness of representative government.

15 | Election Timetables

Candidates and campaign managers will find this chapter interesting. The casual reader will perhaps be disappointed because there is little glamour in the hard work required to win elections.

The campaign commences when the candidate decides to run for public office. The odds will always favor the candidate who knows what he is going to do eighteen months or two years in advance of the day when the decision must be made public. But since most campaigns lack this advantage, the information presented here is applicable to a nine- or ten-month period.

Step 1: Select a campaign manager. It is not necessary to make any public announcement. In fact it will be wise to withhold any public statement about a campaign organization until the candidate makes his formal declaration to the press and other media.

Step 2: Authorize the campaign manager to enlist the group of specialists who will actually be conducting the campaign efforts.

Step 3: Read the election law. Ask a competent lawyer to give you a digest of his opinion of the requirements. Be sure that you know the filing date, the required filing fees if any, petition requirements if nomination is done by petition, restrictions against spending, and requirements for identification on campaign literature. Remember it is a federal offense to put out literature in an election for a federal office which is not clearly identified as to authorship. This doesn't mean that all of your literature has to come from your official campaign sources. You can have numerous committees with innocent identities, but the literature must be identified.

Step 4: Create the research department and put it to work on the possible opponent or opponents, on the history of recent elections, on the development of resource material, on the probable issues.

Step 5: Commence enlisting the Cell Group.

Step 6: Recruit the advisory board or resource team who will help brainstorm the strategy and analyze the opposition.

Step 7: Have the campaign photographs taken. Candidates become very weary—this reflects in their appearance. A photo made eight or nine months in advance of the day of decision will be an honest representation of the candidate. Don't use a picture made three or five or ten years ago. Instruct the photographer to capture the qualities in the candidate which will be emphasized during the campaign.

Step 8: Appoint a treasurer and a finance chairman. Make sure that both of these important assistants clearly understand the election laws. If the treasurer has available an expert bookkeeper, so much the better. There are many campaign expenses which need not be reported. But accurate books, reflecting contributions and expenditures, must be kept. The pitfalls here are too many to be enumerated. They vary from state to state. Improper records or inadequate reporting can disqualify a victor. The finance chairman's primary job is to raise money. The treasurer's job is to make sure that money is accounted for and expended at the direction of the campaign manager.

Step 9: Assemble the full team and start them thinking about the candidate, about his opponent and about the issues.

Step 10: Order the billboards. If your candidate has not made a public announcement, buy the space in the name of some commercial firm whose ownership is friendly to your candidate. (In Oregon I once bought 300 billboards, ostensibly for the Volkswagen automobile. In Arizona we placed our orders in the name of an ice company.) Do whatever is necessary to have the billboards committed at least eight months in advance.

Step 11: Buy your television time. As election day approaches, the available TV time will be in great demand. By placing your order seven or eight months in advance, you can probably secure good segments for the week before election. And if there is to be an effort to secure simulcast scheduling, it must be done well in advance. The five-minute daytime and spots can all be ordered at a much later period, but the good 30-minute availabilities are limited, and unless a request is put in well in advance, the chances are your candidate will not be on TV under the most favorable circumstances during the final two weeks of the campaign.

Step 12: Move your candidate through the constituency. If he is not presently holding public office, schedule him as a speaker at some civic or community project. But start to build the exposure which will be necessary.

Step 13: Develop a campaign budget. At this point the manager should have a fair understanding of what is required. Money can be committed in lump sums to various media, the operation of the campaign group, rent for headquarters, telephones, etc.

Step 14: Pick the day to open the campaign—remember the public memory is short. The days between Labor Day and election day are adequate for the full-scale public campaign, provided adequate preparation has been made in the preceding months.

Step 15: Plan your campaign literature. It may be you will need two or three short pamphlets. Remember that no one really wants to read campaign literature. It must be attractive, adequately illustrated and to the point. If the constituency varies in its economic, political, social and educational attitudes, you will probably need more than one leaflet. Every written piece should have time to cool before it goes into print. If preparations are made well in advance, the campaign manager will not find himself stealing time from some important current necessity to review the proofs of the campaign printed matter.

Step 16: Order your window stickers or bumper strips. If you give the printer adequate time, he will do a better job and you will avoid the possibility of a delay, an improperly printed strip or stickers that won't stay stuck. Give yourself sufficient time to do the whole job over again if necessary.

Step 17: Develop your candidate's campaign itinerary and stay with it. Don't overload him. Don't let travel time requirements consume those hours when he should be appearing before the people.

Step 18: Now establish the time schedule for the public campaign. Plan the activities of the first four weeks and make sure they accelerate every day. Now ask this question: can we maintain acceleration?

Step 19: Start all over again and plan the activities for the final week. Fill every hour of each day. Now work backwards. Reduce the number of activities or appearances in that period two weeks before election day. By scheduling backwards it will become apparent that in the first few days of the campaign one major appearance and one or two visits to small communities will be sufficient.

Step 20: Sit down with the advertising people and allocate the media money. Instruct your agency to produce every possible television film and radio transcription in advance of the opening date of the campaign. If you do this, you will have a relaxed, confident, refreshed candidate. If you postpone making video tapes or the films until the middle of the active season, you are likely to have a tired and lackluster candidate.

Put a deadline on all these plans—August 1. By this time you should have the results of the issue response from the Cell Group, the image surveys, and you should know where the ducks are. You should have an intimate understanding of your opponent and you can plan the real strategy—the series of important home run balls your candidate is going to hit.

If you plan to use the telephone, organize your task force now. Assign volunteers to putting telephone numbers beside the names of those who are registered in your party. This is a tedious, time-consuming task, but the volunteers will do it cheerfully provided you give them ample time to accomplish the work. Remember it takes four weeks for the telephone company to put in the extra lines you will need for a Foot Soldier campaign or for a Get-Out-The-Vote campaign.

When all this preliminary work is done—the charts have been made, the tapes and the films all cut—commence looking for blind-alley issues . . . any questions that can be raised which may possibly divert your opponent from what should be the mainstream of his strategy.

Prepare instructions for the volunteers who will ask eagerly: "What can I do to help?" Remember to assign a specific chore within the competency of all volunteers and put an element of accountability into your request. Volunteers truly want to work but they need direction to be effective. And unless a report is required, some of them will postpone their efforts and you will have gaping holes in your planned coverage.

The campaign group should be meeting at least once a week by August 1. The feedback from the Cell Group should be reviewed with the Advisory Board. The transcribed radio and pre-filmed television should be reviewed by the Advisory Board. Listen attentively to everyone's opinion. When all the reports are in and all the opinions have been registered, the candidate and the campaign manager must sit down and make their decisions. Once the active campaigning starts, there is very little room for improvisation.

I have made up dozens of calendars for campaign managers. In almost every instance they have departed from the calendar under the pressure of local circumstances. But without the calendar, it is doubtful that very many of the necessary chores would have been performed. There are a number of aspects to campaigns which can be planned in advance and need not ever be changed.

Media purchased before the campaign opens and adequately scheduled will hold up through any campaign. The message may be substituted to meet some new threat or to take advantage of some new opportunity, but the exposure, as planned, should remain constant.

The campaign itinerary should never be changed except for the most urgent of reasons. A great deal of effort is required to prepare a coffee or a public meeting and it will take twice as much effort to make explanations and soothe ruffled feathers if a planned appearance is cancelled.

The issues developed in the early portion of the campaign will rarely change and by sticking by those which are truly germane, the planned campaign contributes to a growing confidence on the part of the candidate as he deals with these issues.

One final word about money: get it early, get as much as you can and never commit a dollar which is not in the campaign till.

With a little bit of luck, a great deal of hard work and a sincere dedication to the task, the planned campaign with an adequate candidate will produce a victory. In some cases, victory is not possible. Here defeat can be accepted, but the candidate and manager who lose a campaign because they failed to plan, to assess the opposition correctly, to make provision for contingencies, to enlist the support of a knowledgeable advisory group, will never be able to forgive themselves for their failure.

16 | For Men of Good Conscience

In this small volume on *How To Win An Election* we have moved from the world of casual citizenship into the harsh domain of practical politics. Those who have never before considered the preparation and labor required to win a political contest may be inclined to question the wisdom of political judgments. The best man does not always win. Scoundrels and saints have served this nation in positions of public trust. But for all its imperfections, the system has worked and worked successfully.

The great virtue in representative government is to be found in those provisions which call for a constant reassessment of the validity of the public choice. Our institutions and our elected officials are constantly on trial. Our system still allocates sovereignty to the individual citizen. Victory at the polling place is tentative and temporary. On both the day before and the day after election the world of the victor and the vanquished is filled with uncertainty.

The successful candidate must face an entirely new and frequently frightening responsibility. The excitement and the elation over victory is fleeting. In return for his certificate of successful election, the candidate must forever surrender his right to privacy. Now he belongs to the public—to those who voted against him as well as to those who voted for him.

The loser in a political contest, stinging from defeat, suffers an immediate pain which is not inflicted upon the victor. There is a loss of self-confidence, an inevitable feeling that his friends were not loyal, the bitter reflection over what might have been, the frequent late-blooming knowledge that his defeat was produced not because his opponent was superior, but because of his own blunders in strategy or planning.

Then there is the perplexing, perpetual question: Shall he try again? Should he bind up the financial wounds, the shattered ego and the broken promises and do it all over again?

Losing an election contest—with all its pain—is a profitable experience. For the loser, more surely than the winner, has identified his true friends.

Abraham Lincoln lost several elections before he won the Presidency. Richard Nixon won every election until he lost for the Presidency.

There is no infallible balance upon which the eternal values of victory or defeat may be weighed. We must confess there is bitterness and pain in victory and sweetness and consolation in defeat.

The price of political decision is that some must lose and some must win. Measured against the eternal problems of all mankind, the cost in human disappointment is small. For what all men must seek is a just and ordered society where the instrumentalities of government are used not to enrich or to punish but to advance the relationship of each man to his neighbor in a manner which contributes to the ultimate dignity and responsibility of all men.

If political victory brings responsibility, political defeat should engender charity. No political candidate, no political party has a monopoly on virtue or patriotism. Our task is to support the democratic decisions of this Republic. Where we believe those decisions to be in error, we should labor to reform them. Where we believe them to be right, we should support them. Where they are weak, we should strengthen them.

For many candidates success requires a change of residence from their home to the State Capitol or from their home state to the National Capitol. Old friends are left behind, familiar supports of prior years are withdrawn. New loyalties intrude . . . the public business and the public interest must come ahead of family, hobbies, business or profession.

The corporate jungle where ambitious men are constantly striving to climb the ladders of success by stepping on the shoulders of the less agile or the unwary has been adequately pictured in many novels.

In the political world where men compete for the voters' favor, the clawing and the scratching is persistent. Jealousy and contention within the candidate's party structure will require him to reach decisions in a cold, friendless vacuum.

The successful politician, whatever the new role he has won, will immediately be confronted with a disturbing, hitherto unfamiliar temptation. Theodore Roosevelt once said: "The patriot's first duty is to get himself re-elected." But how far should a man go? George Washington, at the Constitutional Convention, said: "If to please the people we offer what we ourselves disapprove, how can we afterward defend our work?"

A man in the Congress of the United States must constantly find that thin dividing line between pork-barrel, vote-getting legislation and genuine national interest. Friends will impose upon him, and friendship is not something to be dismissed lightly. There will inevitably be long periods of separation from family. His critics will seize upon every mistake as an opportunity to question his veracity, his wisdom and his patriotism.

Men elected to the Congress enjoy the power and perquisites but they must also make a sacrifice. The world of Washington, D.C. is indeed cruel for this is a city of judgment incapable of rendering judgment. The successful candidate who imagined the campaign was bitter and merciless will discover the antagonisms, the petty conniving and the constant undercutting is now a regular part of the pattern of his life.

We require that our governmental servants divorce themselves from the practical world of commerce. We insist that, like Caesar's wife, they must be above suspicion. Yet, the structure of our government places these newly elected servants in a situation where their integrity is constantly under pressure. Some men have made themselves rich through governmental service. Many honest men have been unjustly criticized for accepting small gifts or services. When betrayals of public trust are revealed, we invariably hear an outcry for new legislation to make men good or honest. This is often urged by men who apparently believe in a double standard of morality—one for public service, another for private endeavor.

The winner in a political contest pays a high price for victory. Friends who once dealt with him frankly now fall into that insidious pattern of hero worship. He will find it difficult to hear the truth and almost impossible to separate honest criticism from partisan detraction.

No matter what the victory, the winner will become an immediate target for the opposition press. His personal imperfections will be spread in headlines before his constituents. If he is tired and says the wrong thing, no one will make excuses. Some of his friends and supporters will demand favors in return for the support they gave him at election time. He will be embarrassed in a thousand ways by individuals who truly wish him well. From the moment the first returns are in, he is compelled to worry about the results of the next election.

Most men elected to public office are not independently wealthy. After two, four or six years away from their businesses or their professions, they recognize the difficulties involved in starting over again in private life. Re-election becomes almost a necessity. There is a certain amount of fame to victory. The ego is supported by the knowledge that "I won," but fame is fleeting.

Voters are very apt to adopt the attitude expressed in that question: "What have you done for me lately?"

Abraham Lincoln, on the occasion of his departure from Illinois to become President, spoke on behalf of all men who win elections and enter public service when he said:

> My Friends:
>
> No one, not in my situation, can appreciate my feeling of sadness at this parting. To this place, and the kindness of these people, I owe everything. Here I have lived a quarter of a century, and have passed from a young to an old man. Here my children have been born, and one is buried. I now leave, not knowing when or whether ever I may return, with a task before me greater than that which rested upon Washington. Without the assistance of that Divine Being who ever attended him, I cannot succeed. With that assistance, I cannot fail. Trusting in Him who can go with me, and remain with you, and be everywhere for good, let us confidently hope that all will yet be well. To His care commending you, as I hope in your prayers you will commend me, I bid you an affectionate farewell.